"HOOKED ON BOOKS"

The program described in this book concerns itself primarily with the attitude toward reading and writing of the student who is usually classified as "general" in high school. Such a student's literacy is often marginal and he is customarily credited by his teachers with having a "practical" mind: that is, he needs to perceive and be able to judge the immediate relationship between cause and effect before he can be successfully motivated. His questions about literature are often put in terms of "What does it mean to me?" which is only a more specific version of his questioning answer "Why should I?" to the demands of reading and writing. The purpose of the program called "English In Every Classroom" is to help the men and women who teach such students to supply them with answers which will satisfy their questions and their needs.

HOOKED ON BOOKS

By
DANIEL N. FADER, Ph.D.
and
Morton H. Shaevitz, Ph.D

A BERKLEY MEDALLION BOOK
Published by
BERKLEY PUBLISHING CORPORATION

For Ivan Ludington, without whose
charity there would have been no
story to write.

BERKLEY MEDALLION EDITION, MAY, 1966

*BERKLEY MEDALLION BOOKS are published by
Berkley Publishing Corporation
15 East 26th Street, New York, N. Y. 10010*

Berkley Medallion Books ® TM 757,375

Printed in the United States of America

My Evaluation

I think i have learned a great many more thing here which i will need on the outside to better my self. When i first came seven months ago i could have died from bore, because it was a boring thing to come every day and don't do one thing. But now i believe that this place can be a wonderful place to get boys who have drop out of school back on the track. See when a boy haven't been to school in a long time like i have it is very hard on him anyway to adjust to this program because this whole program is based on school. But after awhile you start thinking about what will i do. Or where will i work when i get out. And it all adds up and you finds out that you will need an eduaction. An eduaction now adays is needed very badly and without one, you are lost.

Well i have found myself and i really belivie that i am going to make good of my self. I have also learned how to communicate with others and i find that this will be very imporante, and also i know how to make my on decision and i will be doing that the rest of my life. I only hope that the decisions i make from now on will be the right ones and yet ill never know. Well Mr. Williams i hope ill see you somewhere on the outside, and ill do very good in Social Studies for you.

Well thanks for every thing.

CONTENTS

PREFACE

Hogman was sweating and so was I. The morning was hot, and we had hundreds of paperbound books to unload from the rear of my Volkswagen sedan. Why hadn't we boxed them before putting them into the car? Why my car? Why me at all—a teacher of English Literature, a lover not a mover of books. We talked as we waited for the cartons.

"That a mighty tiny sheen," he said.

"Mighty tiny," I said, looking at the pile of books filling up the rear.

"Them's tiny books," he said, asking me to talk.

"We get any of yours?" I asked. The principal of the school and I had spent two hours in Cottage Unit A searching the boys' rooms for books. Those we had found were now sprawled in the back of the car. Hogman had come with us from the Cottage, where he had helped to collect the books and load them into the car.

"Had all them James Bondys, but I done read 'em a couple times."

"We get anything you weren't done with?"

"I reckon."

"What?"

"The chuck what makes hisself into a splib."

"Black Like Me?"

"That the one."

I reached back and shuffled through the pile until I found one of the many reclaimed copies of Griffin's book. "Here. Bring it back when you're done."

His chin ducked and he half turned his big body away from me. Then he took the book and slipped it into his back pocket. We were both sweating through our shirts, but he didn't have to be back in Ann Arbor to give a two o'clock lecture. I was thinking about that lecture when Hogman turned toward me, a broad smile on his face, and said kind of low and chuckly, "Like reading, man. You know—it ain't so bad."

You know, it ain't. The program for teaching English in the public schools, contained within the pages of this book, is based upon the notion that reading ain't so bad and it's time more people learned how good it is. Since everybody agrees that people never learn better than when they're children, this book describes a school program suitable in some measure to all children in all American school systems from the kindergarten through the twelfth grade. Though suitable to all, this program is particularly concerned with the student whom educators have identified as "general," meaning all too often that the school system has few specific programs to satisfy his educational needs. This is the same student who can sometimes be identified as disadvantaged and can more often be characterized as impoverished. He is disadvantaged if he is poor, but he may be impoverished and be rich. He is impoverished if he does not read with pleasure, because if he does not read with pleasure then he is unlikely to read at all. And the poorest man in the world is the man limited to his own experiences, the man without books.

Big Bill, Superduck, Hogman, Lester—all were students in the W.J. Maxey Boys Training School at Whitmore Lake, Michigan, a few miles north of Ann Arbor. Their routes to the school were as varied as the faces of poverty; but if their pasts were various, their futures were alike: 75% would return to Maxey or to another penal institution, whether State or federal, juvenile or adult. They spoke of Jacktown (Jackson, Michigan, State Penitentiary) like an old and reliable acquaintance. They were boys, they were old men, they were tough, they couldn't fight their way out of a Girl Scout meeting. Sometime during the first weeks of my work at the school I said to one of the P.E. teachers, "You must get some pretty fair athletes out here." I'll never forget his answer:

"These boys ain't good at nothing. If they was, they wouldn't be here."

I watched them fight. He was right—they didn't have anything but hate going for them. Awkward right-handed

10

leads from flat-footed stances; long, looping punches that landed, when they landed, on shoulders and tops of heads. More than one teacher and cottage supervisor told me that he'd just as soon let them fight because they seldom hurt each other anyway. Basketball, football, softball—sadball. They were society's losers. Worst of all, they saw themselves as having no value. The hate they had as their sometime ally was as likely to be directed against themselves as against others. "Man, what's the use?" The words were engraved on their lips.

On this hot September morning, Leon Holman—principal of the Maxey School—and I—Daniel Fader, Assistant Professor of English at the University of Michigan—were holding a shakedown. Criminals' cells and delinquents' rooms have, in the history of penal institutions, been shaken down for everything from money and drugs, to knives, guns, files, and blunt instruments, but this may have been the first time they were shaken down for books. The wingman went ahead of us, unlocking the doors; Hogman came along behind, pushing the cart. We knew we'd find books, but we never thought it would be like this. Books were everywhere: on their shelves, on their desks, their beds, their washstands. Their teachers said they were reading; the books they carried with them, stuffed in their pockets, said they were reading; the number of books missing from the library said they were reading . . . but here, suddenly, was evidence we couldn't question. It was a perversely happy two hours for both of us, faced as we were with the stolen evidence of our program's success.

That program is described in this book. It concerns itself primarily with the attitude toward reading and writing of the student who is usually classified as "general" in high school. Such a student's literacy is often marginal and he is customarily credited by his teachers with having a "practical" mind: that is, he needs to perceive and be able to judge the immediate relationship between cause and effect before he can be successfully motivated. His questions about literature are often put in the terms of "What does it mean to me?" which is only a more specific version of

11

his questioning answer "Why should I?" to the demands of reading and writing. The purpose of the program called "English In Every Classroom" is to help the men and women who teach such students to supply them with answers which will satisfy their questions and their needs.

This approach to learning is designed to provide the general student with motivation for reading and writing even as it provides him with appropriate materials upon which to practice and with which to reinforce his literacy. Its potential significance to education lies in its systematic expansion of what good English teachers have done or tried to do or wanted to do in schools and classrooms everywhere: convince their colleagues in all subjects that English must be taught by each teacher in every classroom and provide materials for teaching literacy which invite the general student to learn.

All aspects of the curriculum proceed upon the assumption that the chief problem in teaching literacy is not the problem of intellect but the problem of motivation. The program further assumes that in the teaching of literacy, as in the teaching of all other skills, the student's desire to learn makes learning probable.

Members of the Departments of English and Psychology and of the School of Education at the University of Michigan have been engaged for the past two years in shaping and testing a curriculum for the teaching of English in the W. J. Maxey Boys Training School at Whitmore Lake, Michigan. The English program at the Maxey School, which is now also being implemented under experimental conditions in the Garnet-Patterson Junior High School in Washington, D.C., is the source of methods for teaching English described in these pages. That this may be the first school-wide approach to the language problems of the general student says something for the acute nature of the need in that area. Equally revealing is a discovery made by the psychologists who are responsible for testing the program: Within the varied and subtle spectrum of devices invented and validated for the testing of literacy, almost no work at all has been done in the vast area of testing *atti-*

12

tudes toward reading and writing. The implications of this discovery are remarkable.

In the modern history of education, attitudes of readers and writers toward the processes of reading and writing have been regarded—if they have been considered at all —as no more important than the attitude of any mechanical object to the work it performs. Who would ask if a computer likes its work? or if a can opener likes the act of opening or the can it opens? These analogies can be viewed as exaggerations only if we are willing to make two assumptions: that American educators believe most children to be well disposed toward reading and writing; and that they believe these children will so continue independently of the methods and materials used to teach them. No alternate explanation is available. Either the reader/writer is like a mechanical device, to be rated in terms of the relation between input and output (performance), or educators have believed that attitude does not really matter very much after all. One apparent resolution of this unhappy choice was offered me by the former chairman of one of Michigan's largest and most successful (very large percentage of graduates doing well in college) high school English departments: "Reading and writing are *necessary,* don't you see. If we get the performance up, we *know* we've got a child with the right attitude."

This is the same man who gave me information he knew I would be glad to have in my role as Accreditation Visitor in English for the University: *His* staff of English teachers was so cooperative and sensible that he had been called upon only once to ban their use of a book—*The Catcher in the Rye.* But of course we *both* understood about *that.* Though in fact we both did understand about *that,* we both did not understand about attitude. Attitude only follows performance where children are performance-oriented, and even with such children the attitude may not be the one that educators intend to foster. When reading and writing are made means to the end of school success, what happens to performance-oriented children when that success has been attained? To put the question another way, what happens when the performing child becomes the

13

school-graduated (performance-certified) adult? As any librarian or book-seller will tell us, the average modern adult avoids bookstores and libraries as though they were leprosaria. Had the goal of modern, performance-oriented education been the creation of unwilling readers and writers, it could not better have succeeded. All the supporting evidence is bottom-rooted in front of television screens across the nation.

If this is true of the performance-oriented child, what of the child whose environment and training aim him elsewhere? I am using the phrase "performance-oriented" to describe the (usually) middle class child who is taught that time-saving, orderliness, and self-control, all elemental in the process of gratification deferment, will lead him to eventual joy. But what of the (usually) lower class child whose ethics make "live for tomorrow" a joke today? His causes must have very immediate effects, and the devil (who has a school text in his hand) take the foremost. What of this child, to whom "performance-orientation" generally has implied mediocrity and too often has meant failure? At least one part of the answer is clear: We must first re-evaluate our goals as educators before we can hope better to profit our students. In the case both of performance-and other-oriented children, we must bring ourselves to admit that performance-orientation is not now—and probably never has been—enough. We must take careful and unremitting aim at the child's *attitude* before we can expect to see any lasting effect upon his performance. The plan for teaching English which is introduced here takes the child's attitude as its primary, and sometimes its sole object.

THE PROGRAM

"English In Every Classroom" describes an approach to learning which is based upon the dual concepts of SATURATION and DIFFUSION. The first of these key concepts, SATURATION, considers the influence of the child's total school environment upon any attempt to give him functional literacy. It proposes to so surround the student with newspapers, magazines, and paperbound books that he comes to perceive them as pleasurable means to necessary ends. The advantages inherent in selecting such materials for classroom use are very great. First, and most important, all newspapers, most magazines, and the great majority of paperbound books are written in the knowledge that commercial disaster is the reward for creating paragraphs that people *should* read. With the choice a clear one between market success and business failure, publishers, editors, and writers have made their own survival dependent upon discovering what people *will* read. This program advances the radical notion that students are people and should be treated accordingly when being induced to learn how to read. Therefore the obvious choice of newspapers, magazines, and paperbound books as texts for the classroom.

A second and perhaps equally important advantage in the selection of such materials to saturate the student's school environment is their relationship to the world outside the school building. No one believes that we are training children from any social level to be performers in school; every one believes that students come to the schools to learn skills they will need when they leave school, no matter what the level at which they leave. And yet, instead of importing materials from that world for the teaching of the literacy that world requires, we ignore such materials as unworthy of the better world we teachers are dedicated to creating. This program yields to none in its

15

desire to help make a better world. It is equally strong, however, in its desire to educate students to deal with the world as it is. No literature better represents that world than the various periodicals and softbound books which supply the basic materials for the SATURATION program.

The third advantage of these materials is closely related to the second. Not only do newspapers, magazines, and paperbound books *enable* the student to deal with the world as it is, they also *invite* him to do so. All educators are only too familiar with the school-text syndrome, that disease whose symptoms are uneducated students and unread materials—unread not because of their good quality but because of their bad format. School texts often go unread just because they are school texts and apparently have very little to do with the non-school world. One certain way to break the syndrome is to remove the proximate causes—in this case traditional school texts—and substitute newspapers, magazines, and paperbound books in their place.

SATURATION applies in principle not only to the selection and distribution of periodicals and soft-bound texts throughout the curriculum, but to the explosion of writing in the student's school environment. This explosion is based upon the practice of DIFFUSION, the second of the two key concepts in the design of "English In Every Classroom" and the concept from which the scheme primarily takes its name. Whereas SATURATION refers to the materials used in every classroom to induce the child to enter the doorway of functional literacy, DIFFUSION refers to the responsibility of every teacher in every classroom to make the house of literacy attractive. In discharging this responsibility, every teacher becomes an intermediary between the student and functional literacy. In order that the student may come to view writing as a means to all ends, all ends which he pursues in a scholastic context must insist upon writing as the means through which they can be approached. In short, every teacher becomes a teacher of English and English is taught in every classroom.

WRITING

One of the most interesting yearly statistics made available to many university faculties is the number of incoming freshmen chosen from the top ten percent of their high school classes. The number has recently grown so large at some universities that their faculties are now more concerned with the good students who are excluded than with the poor students who may still be admitted. Though this improvement in quality of the entering class has been nowhere more marked than in Freshman English, the promised land of no Freshman English course is not yet at hand. For in spite of the notable increase in intelligence and accomplishment which characterizes the average freshman, he still writes miserably when he enters the university. Because of his wholly inadequate preparation in composition, he must take an English course designed to teach him how to write at least well enough to survive the four years of his undergraduate experience. There can be little doubt that, at many schools, Freshman English is successful in realizing this aim. The reason for this success is of crucial importance to the establishment of an effective program for teaching reading and writing to public school students.

That Freshman English is usually very effective is partially attributable to the quality and predisposition of its students. But these are also the same students who learn so little about English composition before their first semester at the university that a course like Freshman English becomes necessary to their collegiate survival. What then effects so powerful a change in their performance as writers during their initial collegiate semester? The answer is embarrassingly simple—for the first time in their school experience, they write. They write a small mountain of out-of-class papers, in-class papers, exercises, paragraphs, sentences . . . they write and they write and they write. With very few exceptions, they write more in one semester

17

than they have written before in one lifetime. And, unremarkably enough, they learn how to write. They have, in short, learned to write through the one method they have never before been subjected to, the one method which can be expected to succeed—the constant practice of writing itself.

This view of the dynamics of the learning process in Freshman English is twice relevant to the proposals found in this program of reading and writing. The proximate relevance of the Freshman English experience at the university to the teaching of writing in the public schools is of course the relationship of the practice of writing to the learning of writing skills at both institutions. The ultimate relevance of the experience, however, is both more important and less apparent: Freshmen students at the university in effect teach themselves how to write. Though the teacher and his texts are important, the only indispensable element is the continuous prose output of the student himself. He is asked to do what he has always been capable of doing; soon he finds that he rather likes the experience, for the task has been tailored to his measure. The typical freshman student likes his English class, he likes to write (though he probably doesn't know it), and he's able to produce ten thousand words of deathless prose for one class in one semester. In all of these predispositions and abilities he is likely to be very different from his public school counterpart, who too often barely endures his English class and is sometimes stricken by mental paralysis at the very thought of having to write for any reason. Where the proximate relevance of the Freshman English experience to teaching English in the public schools is likely to be the positive correlation between learning to write and the act of writing for both groups of students, the ultimate relevance of the experience is a thoroughly negative correlation: The university freshman learns much from his English class because his previous verbal experiences and developed aptitudes combine to predispose him favorably to the English-class situation; many public school students learn little from the English class because their previous experiences and verbal disabilities conspire to cause them to reject any learning experience named "English." If this argument is valid, then the three following propositions are significant: (1) The public school student may be taught to write by writing (in quantities and on subjects appropriate to his individual level of attainment); (2) This teaching and writing must not be confined to the English classroom which has so often been for him a scene of failure and a source of frustration; (3) The nature of the English classroom must be radically altered if it is to play a meaningful part in his education.

On the basis of these three propositions, certain conclusions seem inevitable: The teaching of English in the public school should be viewed as the primary responsibility of the English teacher and as a secondary responsibility of every other teacher with whom the student has regular classroom contact. This division of responsibility, with its resultant diffusion of reading and writing throughout the entire curriculum, should have a number of salutary effects, most important being communication to the student of the sense that reading and writing can be as natural to his existence as walking and talking. His previous experience has assured him that only English teachers demand constant proof of his literacy; he can hardly avoid learning the lesson that reading and writing are special functions reserved for special occasions, in this case the English class, and that they have no unavoidable, normative relationship to the rest of his world. It is to the purpose of dispelling that damaging illusion that this recommendation is made.

Implementation of the practice of shared responsibility for the student's training in English has proven not only relatively easy in the Maxey Boys Training School and the Garnet-Patterson Junior High School, but also unexpectedly pleasant for the faculties involved. When I first met with the full faculties of the Maxey and Garnet-Patterson schools for three day training seminars in August of 1964 and 1965, respectively, I was uncomfortably aware on both occasions of how cold a welcome my program might receive. For the program proposes an approach to the teaching of literacy which challenges two of the dearest and most ancient misconceptions of the profession. These are the myths, customarily paired for strength, of the teacher as individualist and the classroom as castle. Together they have done more harm to the profession of teaching than any other combination of ideas or events. The myth of the teacher as individualist serves for example; because of that myth, because of the mental set it represents, meaningful cooperation amongst teachers is essentially non-existent. Each teacher is so concerned to perpetuate the values and conditions of his own preparation, so concerned to protect his feudal rights as a freeman, that he effectively isolates himself from his peers. Teachers have *no* peer group in the functional sense of that term. They may attend professional classes, take courses during the academic year and during the summer, but they tend to be speakers and auditors of monologues rather than participants in dialogues. *They do not profit from each other* because they are the true inheritors of the modern theory of compartmentalized education, a theory which declares each man sufficient unto his subject and each subject sufficient unto itself. General practitioners are as little respected and as meagerly rewarded in teaching as they are in medicine.

Inevitably corollary to the idea of teacher as individualist is the theory of classroom as castle. Without the second, the first could hardly be as destructive as it is. Part of our feudal inheritance is the notion that a man's home is his castle. Sanctified in the home by law and custom, this theory has become a practice imitated in the schools. Like most imitations, the shape of the thing has undergone subtle change. Whereas in the home a man has the freedom *to* order his life and raise his family, in the classroom this tradition has been interpreted as freedom *from*. Rather than exercising freedom *to* experiment and freedom *to* criticize (both self and colleagues), teachers distinguish themselves by the process of in-gathering which frees them *from* self-and-peer criticism to a degree foreign to any other profession. I would be the last to deny that public criticism—often reflecting only the ignorance and prejudice of the critics—has given teachers one very good reason for insulating themselves from further shocks. But the reaction has built a thickness of insulation which has become a burden rather than a protection: Teachers now suffer most from their inability to hear each other.

The program I proposed to the faculties of both schools asked them to hear and to help each other. Within this program, each English teacher at Maxey and at Garnet-Patterson became the leader and servant of a team of teachers and every teacher except the Physical Education instructors became a team member. Teams have been formed as much as possible by grouping an English teacher with the other instructors of that teacher's pupils. Where because of varied curriculum in the public school (foreign language instruction, for example) such grouping is not completely feasible, teachers of subjects other than English are assigned to the team which instructs the majority of their students. Teams meet weekly in the Garnet-Patterson School and less often at Maxey, where the teachers have now had almost two years of work within the program. These weekly meetings are meant at first to be supplemented by and—as in the Maxey School—eventually to be replaced by the personal interaction of the English teacher with individual members of his team. In order that the English teacher may have sufficient time to devote to coordination of team effort, he is assigned one class less than the school's normal teaching load. Where an English Department chairman is designated, he is relieved of a second class in order to coordinate team teaching efforts and materials distribution throughout the school.

Team teaching is an old phrase which this plan hopes to invest with new meaning. In return for lightened classroom responsibility, each English teacher acts as a resource person and a guide for his colleagues in the diffusion of English throughout every classroom in the school. He assists each member of his team to set up a writing schedule which produces at least one piece of writing every other day in all subjects other than English. Writing in mathematics class about processes of arithmetic or practical applications of algebra; writing in shop or art classes about particular skills and necessary procedures; writing in science classes about the physical nature of his environment—all these occasions serve not only to make the student master of a significant portion of his verbal world, but also to reinforce his special knowledge of that particular subject. Since in this view of the English curriculum the frequency of written exercises is far more important than their length, they vary from a few sentences to an occasional page. They are never unpleasantly long, they are not always read, and their grammar and rhetoric is not corrected by the subject instructor unless he strongly desires to do so.

First, let me explain the unusual practice of requiring students to write papers that no instructor will read: The real purpose of written exercises in all divisions of the curriculum is not so much to get students to write correctly as it is simply to get them to write. The radical aspect of this approach to teaching English does not lie in some Utopian notion of making prose stylists of all public school students. Its real innovation is that it depends far less upon the teacher and far more upon the student than do more traditional methods of teaching writing. Instead of a few papers covered with his own corrections, the teacher has many papers at least partially covered with students' prose. Of the five sets of papers received in every two week period by instructors in subjects other than English, one set per week is read and commented upon for content by the class instructor, one set every two weeks is passed on by him to the students' English teacher who corrects grammar and rhetoric, and one set each week is filed *unread* in the students' folders. This treatment of one set of papers each week in every classroom recognizes and encourages the idea that the practice of writing may be distinguished from its performance. It offers the student opportunity to condition himself for performance by allowing him time to exercise his writing muscles. Disposing of one set of papers each week without either reading or correcting them serves as a constant reminder to English teacher and subject teacher alike of the real purpose of these continuing exercises—to develop the student's prose-writing muscles to the point where he can use them without fear of aches and strains. Until this point is reached, practice will continue to be far more beneficial to the student than correction.

The idea of unread papers has long been rejected in American education on the basis of the myth that "children must have some tangible evidence that their efforts are appreciated or they won't work." That this unchallengeable truism ever came to be translated into the notion that everything a student writes must be read, or otherwise he won't write, is a tribute to the illogical capacities of the human mind. The unsurprising fact is that a child can be taught to practice writing, both in the classroom (brief papers) and outside of it (the journal), just as he can be taught to practice a musical instrument or an individual sport. Just as in music and sports, the key to practice in writing is expectation: Our experience at both the Garnet-Patterson and Maxey schools has been that even the worst students take some pleasure in the idea of uncorrected writing when they have been conditioned to expect and value their freedom to practice.

I would like to emphasize here that this approach to the teaching of English does not envision making English teachers of instructors trained in other specialties. It recognizes that in the best of all possible worlds instructors of all subjects will perceive the partial dependence of their disciplines upon the verbal adequacy of their students, and will take appropriate steps to insure that adequacy. Until such a millennium is upon us, however, this program is built upon the expectation that no teacher other than the English teacher will correct the grammar and rhetoric of student papers, but that all teachers will be encouraged to make simple corrections where the necessity of such corrections may be apparent to them. Since this procedure is dependent upon the good will of the subject instructors who help to effect it, they must not be made to feel uneasy about their own mastery of the language. Much effort has been expended in both schools to make them clearly understand that they may regard their role, if they wish, as that of a passive intermediary between their students on the one hand and functional literacy on the other. In

23

making this clear, great emphasis has been placed upon the *quantitative* importance of these written exercises.

The speed and thoroughness with which teams have formed and begun their work at both the penal and public school have been attributed to a surprisingly narrow range of causes by the teachers and supervisors at both institutions. Foremost in this very brief list is the realization which pervades the faculty of every school with a considerable percentage of students who will terminate their education at the end of high school, if the system can manage to keep them that long. Simply stated, that realization is one of growing failure and lessening hope. In the many public schools I have visited in the past five years, the song of success has always had one part a dirge and one chorus the same: We believe we are reasonably successful in the first three grades with most of our children; we know we are doing moderately well with our bright students at almost all levels and better than that in our college-preparatory and advanced placement work. But our handling of the general student varies from bad to shocking. We need help. Where can we get it? We need help. . . .

Second and last on this list is the school-wide, country-wide sense that the greatest failure in the education of the general student lies in his language preparation. He is so difficult to teach, say teachers from other subject areas, because he is so difficult to communicate with. Stripped of its social implications, this complaint often reduces itself to the basic problem of literacy. The child who can't or won't read or write or listen well cannot be educated in any subject in the school curriculum. Because he is essentially unreachable in every teacher's classroom, and because teachers in every classroom recognize his language deficiencies as a great part of his problem, the majority of his teachers are ready to aid the English teacher in giving him language to deal with his world. That readiness born of frustration on the part of *all* the teachers has played a very large part in leveling the customary barriers that might have impeded the progress of *English In Every Classroom*.

In concluding this section on the teaching of writing as

a responsibility of the entire school faculty, let me cite from the collection accumulated during the past two years of responses to the program by those who have been obliged to teach within it:

"I haven't got time to teach English and Math. You'd better tell me which I'm supposed to do."

"Their vocabulary seems about to have doubled. They really go for those dictionaries."

"I've noticed a big improvement in their history spelling. I don't know if it's due to the program or not."

"I find that the pupils show much greater freedom of expression than they did at the beginning. The papers most recently written are much more interesting to read than the earlier papers."

"I've taught for a long time and I know you can't get kids to write if you don't correct their papers. Their parents would complain too."

"Every member of my team has said how much better our students are writing. It's important to the students that all of their teachers are working on their writing together. They like that."

"It makes the child aware of the consolidated efforts of the teachers."

"It gives the English teacher opportunities to evaluate her own effectiveness by the quality of work done by the child in other classrooms."

"I like the democratic way we plan."

"It's a wonderful method of teaching."

"It stinks."

THE JOURNAL

Of all the many and varied encouragements and inducements to writing offered within the scope of *English In Every Classroom,* none has been more consistently successful than the journal. Far from originating in this program, the journal has been used in other schools before. English teachers and teachers of other subjects have occasionally turned to it as a support for more formal writing assignments. I have seen journals in public schools used for continuing book reports in English classes, for observations upon municipal government in civics classes, and as diaries in social studies classes. Wherever they have been included within the school program, they seem to have pleased teacher and student alike. Taking their own inclinations and their students' pleasure as a guide, the faculties at Maxey and Garnet-Patterson have used the journal with a breadth and freedom not found in other schools.

In addition to the two paperbound books from the library that each entering student is allowed to choose for his own, and the paperbound dictionary he is given to keep, he also receives from his English teacher a spiral notebook to begin the school year. This is identified as his journal, an appropriate name for a notebook intended for daily use by every student. When he is given his journal, the student is told that quantity of production is the only criterion upon which his writing will be judged. Length, content, style, grammar, rhetoric—all are insignificant when compared with the overriding consideration of quantity. This journal, the student is told, has only one reason for existence: to provide you with a field upon which you can practice your writing. You will be required to write not less than a certain number of pages each week (two pages a week presently in both schools), and you will be asked each Thursday to turn in your journal to your English teacher, who will return it on Friday. Your teacher will read your journal only if you invite him to read it. Under no circumstances, however, will your journal be corrected. It will be assessed for quantity and for nothing else.

The process of introducing this comprehensive and quantitative use of the journal into the Garnet-Patterson Junior High School has produced one important modification of practice in the Maxey School: Journals are *read* by the teachers in the public school. This is very different from the procedure of the training school, where the fact that the journal is not read, except by specific invitation, is one of its most attractive aspects from the boys' point of view. Journals may remain unread in the training school because a penal institution, no matter how progressive and enlightened, is still a closed system designed in the first instance to remove the offender from society. Each member of the training school staff teaches and counsels there precisely because he understands that vituperation and obscenity are stages through which disturbed children may pass on their way toward freeing themselves from some of the frustration and fear that shackles them to illiteracy. In the public schools, however, this problem must be handled very differently because of the public nature of all the students' school language, whether spoken or written. The simple expedient of telling the students that their notebooks will be glanced at quickly each week, though neither read carefully nor corrected under any circumstances, largely solves the difficult problem of publicly unacceptable words and ideas.

The quantitative view of writing has as a necessary corollary the permissive handling of journal entries by the teacher. Whether written inside or outside of class, whether legible or barely intelligible, whether a sentence, a paragraph, or a page—each entry is another building block in the structure of the student's functional literacy. If the teacher can bring himself to regard the journal in this way, he will be equally satisfied with prose that is original and prose that is copied from a newspaper, a magazine, or a book. And both he and his students will be more than satisfied with work which is evaluated by no one. If close-coupled with this permissiveness in the nature of the entry is the unvarying weekly check on the amunt of production, then the customary formula for success in all human enterprise—a little license with accompanying obligation—can make the journal an exceptionally useful teaching tool.

Teachers in the program have found that varying the pace of the journal's use by varying its place has been an especially successful teaching stratagem with their students. One teacher alternates weekly periods of using the journal in the classroom for brief writing assignments with equal periods of having his students write outside of class. He has observed that he gets a good deal of personal writing outside of class, but that the diarist in his students recedes into the background when they are called upon to write in their journals in class. Furthermore, he has found that he gets surprisingly creative production related to the day's classroom activities when he reserves the last ten minutes of the hour rather than the first ten for journal writing.

In the early stages of the program at the Maxey School, a disappointingly small number of boys wrote in their journals for more than the required two pages. We had half expected that the journal would be used by many as a kind of private stamping ground where they could work over their enemies, work out their fears, and work at the habit of writing. We were wrong; now, a year and a half later, we know why. The journal became all we had expected it to be, and more, but instead of taking its anticipated and immediate place as a cause of change in the students' attitude, it became rather the effect and result of that change. As language took on a real rather than an imputed value at the school, as speed with a dictionary and ability to write for the school newspaper and literary magazine became means to the end of peer esteem, the average weekly production in the journal increased slowly but surely. This average was increased by action on two fronts: Teachers found it easier to obtain at least the minimum from almost everybody, and more students began to write longer and longer weekly entries. A page a day, once highly remarkable, became more usual, and five pages a day became the average output of one young man who confided in his teacher that he'd written that much in the first fifteen days just to see if the school would really give him another notebook when he filled the first one. It would and did; he's now on his fourth notebook and shows no signs of weakening.

Amongst the many creative uses found for the journal, one of the most interesting is the "good listening" device employed by one of the English teachers. The more this particular teacher spoke with her students, the more she came to believe that though they appeared to understand what she was saying—and, when asked, would claim that they did—they did not in fact customarily understand her spoken directions. With this realization came the inspiration to employ the journal as a dictation workbook in which "listening good" became a challenging pursuit. A few days of this practice every two weeks has become a popular pastime with her students as they concentrate upon reproducing exactly what she is saying. She believes that the interest in her exact words which this exercise fosters carries over into closer attention to her words when interpretation rather than mere transcription is the requirement.

The subject of the journal would not be complete without retelling the story of Lester. Though the name is necessarily false, the story is improbably true: Lester came to the penal school by the surest of several possible routes; he got himself born a Negro. Without that, the odds against his attendance at BTS would have risen enormously. Having managed that, however, he proceeded to increase his chances greatly by growing up in his mother's care in Detroit's Negro ghetto. Get born a Negro, get raised by your mother in Detroit's East Side, and you've done about all you can. The rest is a matter of luck.

Lester had the luck, all of it bad. If you're a White boy from a rural area, you can drag race your car, badmouth the sheriff, and WHAM! BTS. But if you're a Negro or White boy from Detroit, you've got to go some to make the scene at Maxey. Lester went some.

When he arrived at the school, he was sixteen years old and a habitual criminal. He had to be in order to get one of the places reserved for Wayne County boys.

During his stay in the reception center at Whitmore Lake, Lester underwent the testing designed to produce a sufficient paper identity for the juvenile penal authorities to classify and assign him to one of the five available programs throughout the State. The sum of the testing was that Lester was passive, that he would like to be in a school program, and that he functioned on a fourth grade school level at the age of sixteen. With that identity, Lester came to the Maxey School.

Perhaps the experience he remembers most clearly from his first day in class at BTS is the large spiral notebook he was given and the accompanying directions for its use. He remembers being told that he would be expected to write at least two pages a week in that notebook, and that under no circumstances would anyone correct what he wrote.

"Suppose I can't think of two pages worth?" Maybe Lester asked the question. Someone always does.

"Then copy. Copy from a newspaper or a magazine or a book."

"You mean you don't care if we copy?"

"That's right."

"You putting us on."

"Try me."

Try her they would. When you've been told since you've been old enough to write that copying is BAD, copying can be its own reward. The boys copy and they copy *and* they copy. Then they copy some more. The modern, no-holds-barred record for copying at BTS is forty-five pages in the first week; teachers are grateful, however, if they get two. One youngster, who had never read it before, was fascinated by *Time* magazine. For four weeks he copied articles and parts of articles daily from the same well-worn copy. His teacher was delighted. Not only had he written more in that month than he may have written before in a lifetime, but his conversation was full of the things he was reading. During the brief period of four weeks he

30

passed from truculent reserve to something like participation in his English and Social Studies classes.

A few boys with remarkable stamina copy the bulk of their journal work for the entire academic year. Most get tired of copying, however, especially where no teacher renews its attraction by forbidding it. And most go naturally to the next stage of journal usage—the diary. For almost all of the boys this second stage is also the final stage of their journal development. Since both the ability to create and the need to confide are found in about the same proportions in free and incarcerated societies, the journals in the Maxey School are diaristic in the extreme. From diary to friend to comforter and sole confidant is no long step when you think little of humanity in general and even less of yourself. Like the majority of his fellows, Lester filled his journal with the thoughts and transactions of his daily life. Unlike his peers, most of whom do little more than the prescribed two pages each week, Lester wrote and wrote and wrote. Fourth grade attainment on a test validated upon white middle class children by white middle class adults would have meant nothing to him had he known about it. He liked to write; he discovered he liked to write by writing. By writing everything, that is. Even poetry.

At first he copied the poems he found in magazines and newspapers. But not for long. Soon he was writing his own verse. It was not poetry, not yet; but it wasn't doggerel and it wasn't bad. His teacher began to read what he was writing—by invitation. She offered him a few criticisms—again, by invitation. Lester continued to write, his collection of verse grew, and with it grew his self-esteem. He was, for the first time in his life, *creating* something. Not only was it all his, but it was all good. No one said should not, could not, or must not. Approbation. Though he didn't know the word, he began to know the warmth of the feeling. He wanted to publish a magazine of his poetry for the school.

Lester's teacher knew she couldn't say no, but her yes was weak and worried. Lester had come a long way, too long a way to risk losing him to the jeers and taunts of boys

31

for whom poetry is for people who walk with a certain lightness of foot. Reluctantly, with fear and trepidation, because she couldn't say no, she mimeographed the poems and distributed them throughout the school. We held our breath.

Of all the private predictions, varying from hot disaster to cold indifference, none dared to be as hopeful as reality. None of us, barricaded within the assumptions of our middle-class worlds, foresaw the eminence that poetry would bring to Lester at BTS. And we were even less capable of foreseeing the value that Lester's publications would bring to poetry at BTS. One type of book we had omitted completely from our original paperback library at Maxey was the poetry anthology and the book of poetry by a single author. If we were collectively certain of anything, we were sure that these boys had never willingly read poetry in their lives and were unlikely to begin at BTS. We think somewhat less now of the value of collective certainty. Lester's poems were published. Lester was lionized. We were overwhelmed. Lester published two further collections before he completed his stay at Maxey. With each publication, the group's view of Lester and poetry (and Lester's view of himself) changed profoundly. Lester saw something in himself to value, and his peers saw something in poetry. Lester is long gone from Maxey, but the librarian is still having trouble meeting the demand for books of poetry.

What began as an improbable story ends as an impossible fantasy. As Lester underwent the dramatic change from a passive to an aggressive human being, from a local laugh to a local leader, his aspirations changed as well. The world of the W.J. Maxey Boys Training School at Whitmore Lake became even smaller than it was. Lester wanted copyright to his extensive production of poetry. Acting upon the advice of his English teacher, Lester wrote to Congressman Weston Vivian, Democrat, representing Michigan's Second District, of which Whitmore Lake is a part. Lester sent his poems under cover of a letter enquiring about copyright. Mr. Vivian's response was predictable, if you still believe in the Age of Miracles. All this remarkable Congressman did was to read one of Lester's poems into the *Congressional Record,* get Vice-President Humphrey's signature upon a copy of that *Record,* fly to Detroit, motor to Whitmore Lake, and present the autographed copy of the *Record* to Lester at an assembly of the entire school. No one will ever be able to assess accurately what Mr. Vivian's visit did directly for Lester's ego, vicariously for the egos of Lester's peers, and incidentally for the causes of poetry and literacy. The results of that visit are still being tallied a year after the fact.

Because improbability is boundless, Lester's story has another episode. After his release from BTS, Lester called his teacher regularly to report on his activities. A few months after his release I walked into the school library one afternoon to find her staring past the drugstore spinners full of paperbound books, staring at nothing.

"Lester called this morning." I could barely hear the words.

"What's wrong?"

"He says he just got a $500 check from a publisher for his poems."

It was true. Improbable. Impossible. Nevertheless true. Another BTS alumnus who keeps in touch with his former teachers came to visit the school sometime after Lester's telephone call. He was able to verify the story with the best sort of information—he had seen the check. It was no surprise to him: "When that cat come from Washing Town," he told us, "everybody *know* Lester going to be *the man.*"

READING

No student is likely to learn to write if he believes that writing is an affliction visited upon defenseless students solely by English teachers; nor is he likely to learn to read unless reading is made a part of his entire curricular environment. Therefore this program requires that *all* teachers base a significant part of their course content and a portion of their written exercises upon textbooks designed to invite reading. Popular and journalistic, these textbooks are the newspapers, magazines, and paperbound books which import the non-school world into the classroom.

An acceptable text can be negatively defined as one which is not an anthology and does not have hard covers, for the hard-bound text and the anthology have a number of serious defects in common. To the unsuccessful student both are symbols of a world of scholastic failure, and both to some degree are causes of that failure. No hard-bound text was ever thrust into a child's pocket, and no anthology was ever "read" in any meaningful sense of that word by anybody. The student fed upon a steady diet of highly selected collections is not being encouraged to read so much as he is being trained to survey, to mine, and to collect shining nuggets of precious literature. The discrimination he is taught by reading a typical school anthology is greater than it need be, and the actual quantity and continuity of his reading is less than it should be. Such an anthology testifies to a failure of effort or imagination, or both, on the part of the educator, and a surrender of inspiration to convenience. Furthermore, it participates with all other large, hard-cover books in the desk-top-and-locker disease which so often afflicts less easily portable and digestible texts given to poor and mediocre students. Such books were obviously not made to give companionship to immature students; recognizing this, students usually give them the minimal attention they appear to deserve.

In emphasizing the importance of the soft-bound, easily portable text, I wish to point out two great advantages which the use of such texts brings. First, the traditional, confined sense of "text" can and should be expanded to include any appropriate paperbound book and periodical now being published. Certainly the attention given by educators to *what* a child is reading has proven, by its exaggerated emphasis upon "quality," damaging in the extreme to *how much* he reads. Generations of students have grown to scholastic maturity nurtured entirely solely on anthologized and authorized classics, and have become the parents of new generations who, like themselves, are without the habit of reading because the typical school program neither stimulates nor breeds a desire to read in the average student. In teaching all children, but most especially in teaching the environmentally disadvantaged child, attention should be refocussed upon the *quantity* of supervised reading they can accomplish. This argument makes the strongest sort of case for the use of materials which resemble, if they are not actually from, the student's world outside the school and classroom. The greatest possible use should be obtained from newspapers and magazines in every class in all curricula, and soft-bound books should be preferred to hard-bound texts wherever this preference is in any way possible.

The second great advantage of soft-bound, easily portable texts lies in the invitation to possession and casual reading which their very form extends. In many less fortunate children, the need to possess is unusually strong and relatively easy to gratify. Soft-bound books and magazines are an ideal means of satisfying this need, for the full possession of them involves more than the mere actuality of ownership. The physical fact of books and magazines in a child's possession is the most likely method of encouraging that child to read, especially when the reading materials closely resemble those with which he is at least vaguely familiar outside the life of the classroom.

This general discussion of reading precedes a review of

the school library and a detailed analysis of the types and titles of paperbound books which have been successful within this program. Intended as a preface to that review and analysis is the following brief examination of the use of newspapers and magazines in both the penal and public schools:

The most important recommendation of the newspaper, repeated in many forms by the English teachers who have taught from it at least three times a week for periods varying from two months to two years, is that it is *warmly welcomed* by the students who use it. Again and again teachers have said that the newspaper "gives me something to do all the time; I don't have to worry about how I'm going to hold their attention." As any teacher knows who has had to deal with reluctant readers (as which of us has not?), the first step is the most important in moving them toward literacy. Get them willingly to make that initial overture toward reading, and their literacy will be as functional as the fingers that turn the pages.

Occasionally the overture toward reading is played in strident tones, as it was last year in an English class of eight boys at the Maxey School. The teacher had planned the class around the newspaper. The boys had written a paragraph summary of a lead story on the front page, begun a letter responding to a controversy being carried on in "Letters to the Editor," and answered a series of questions about a number of brief articles in the sport pages. They had been subjected to the newspaper for almost an entire hour when the teacher told them that the class was over and the time had come to pass in the newspaper. Their rising growl of protest had brought me quickly down the hall from the library. The sight and sound of eight sixteen- and seventeen-year-old "non-readers" complaining loudly because their English class was over for the day was so unexpected that I stood in the doorway, confused and uncertain, until I saw the smile on the teacher's face. As he said afterward, he knew he should do something beside grin at me, but nothing else seemed to fit his feelings.

The newspaper is no more the answer to a teacher's prayer than any other inanimate teaching tool. But it is a

36

superior tool when coupled with the animating force of the teacher's confident use, because it contains within its pages something to engage and reward the interest of every child. As all novel devices, however, it must be protected from overexposure. The best method we have discovered of protecting the newspaper from itself is to alternate its employment with the magazine. The average we have striven for in the English classes of the Maxey and Garnet-Patterson schools is thrice weekly teaching from newspapers coupled with twice weekly usage of magazines. This frequency model may take a number of different patterns, allowing as it does for alternate daily use of newspaper and magazine or serial use of either type of publication. Most important, however, is the recognition that any tool may have its cutting edge made dull through overuse.

A question often asked is, "What kind of newspaper is best to use?" Implied in the question are two choices—one between a local and a national publication, the other between two or more local newspapers. As for the first implication, the choice between a local and a national publication is usually no choice at all. The purpose of using the newspaper in the classroom is to place before the student materials which are likely to *invite* him to literacy. *The New York Times*, for example, may be in every way superior to the local rag dominated by an editor-publisher who is a moral idiot and a grammar school dropout. Human failure though he may be, he nevertheless fills his paper with local news of every description. Because of this, in the eyes of the reluctant reader he is very likely to have created a more attractive product than any big-city journal, no matter how justly famous.

The choice between local papers is not so easy, implying as it does a value judgment bound to create ill-will if the purchase of newspapers by the school system takes on any considerable size. The presence of more than one newspaper can be a boon rather than a dilemma, however, for two newspapers offer opportunities for comparative study of everything from style to "fact." Practical arguments can be cited for using either the morning or the evening paper. The evening paper is useful because of the time it allows for teachers to review it for teaching purposes. The morning paper is equally useful, this time for the fresher news it contains. Whether published in the morning or evening, however, the newspaper communicates a sense of vitality and immediate excitement equalled by no other public writing of our time. It is just that sense of excitement which has been so sadly missing from the texts of our public schools.

Because the magazine captures the reader's attention in a way quite different from the newspaper, it is an excellent complement to the paper's use in the classroom. Whereas the newspaper does very little to make itself visually attractive, hoping instead that the topical magnetism of its contents will briefly lure the reader, the magazine does much with form and color because of its longer life and the more leisurely reading pace it invites. Magazines have proven extremely successful teaching devices at the Maxey and Garnet-Patterson schools. After much trial and some error, the teachers at both schools have discovered which magazines are most welcome and most useful to their students. Though the list is reasonably exhaustive, it is not exclusive. Other magazines may work as well or better in other circumstances.

One important matter before classifying and listing the titles: how many magazines and newspapers are enough? After a great deal of experimentation with numbers of newspapers, we have discovered that one set of papers per day for each English teacher is a very workable arrangement. The size of the set should be equal to the number of students in the English teacher's largest class, plus one for the teacher. In a public school with 840 students, for example, all of whom are taking English every day in classes of 35, with teachers handling four classes each, six full time English teachers would be required. Each of these teachers would receive 35 papers each morning for her students plus one for herself, a total of 216 papers a day. These papers would be used by the English teacher three times a week in each of her four classes; they would be available to the members of her team for use at all other times. In practice this means that the papers are in use in

38

English classes for about half the teaching periods of the week and may be employed for an equal period of time in all other subjects together.

Magazines can be ordered on the basis of a partially similar formula. For each magazine that the school decides to use, the number of copies purchased should be equal to the number of students in the school's largest homeroom class. This arrangement has worked very well with the exception of a few magazines found to be extraordinarily helpful in teaching unusually slow readers. These are the children's magazines known as *The Golden Magazine, Jack and Jill,* and *The Children's Digest.* In spite of the title of *Jack and Jill,* painfully reminiscent of the world of Dick and Jane, all three magazines are so successful with both teachers and children in the junior high school that we have had to double our purchase of each of them in order to satisfy the demand.

These three publications for children serve to introduce the seven various categories of magazines which have proved both welcome and useful in the schools in which "English In Every Classroom" has been introduced. The other six divisions of the list are composed of picture, news, digest, sports, teenage, and science magazines. These names are used for convenience of grouping; they are not complete descriptions, nor do they always describe discreet groups. *Life* is a very good example: Clearly it is a picture magazine, and it is most valuable for its photographs. On the other hand, it also reports the news and belongs partially to that section of the list as well. *Look* and *Ebony* complete the titles of picture magazines we have used, while *Jet, Newsweek,* and *Time* comprise the news magazines. In addition to *Children's Digest, Negro Digest* and *Reader's Digest* form the group of monthly summaries. *Sport* and *Sports Illustrated; Popular Science, Popular Mechanics,* and *Hot Rod;* and *In* and *Teen* fill the respective categories of sports, science, and teenage publications. Add to these the *Saturday Evening Post,* which fits conveniently into no particular category, and the list of magazines is complete.

Magazine distribution throughout the school is the responsibility of the English chairman in the junior high school and of a selected teacher in the training school where no chairman has been appointed. Both employ approximately the same methods: Teachers are asked to reserve those magazines they know they will want to use on particular days in ensuing weeks. During the week before the reserved magazines are to be used, a list of magazines with unreserved days is circulated throughout the school. When magazines arrive at the school, they are held out of circulation for one or two days in order to allow all teachers to become familiar with their contents. At the end of that period, a final list of available magazines is circulated throughout the school.

The formula for minimal usage—at least twice a week in the English and Social Studies classrooms; at least once a week in every other classroom—guarantees a considerable classroom reading of magazines within the program. But no formula can guarantee *meaningful* usage of materials, no matter how reasonable the formula and how apparently attractive the materials. The success of magazines within the plan of *English In Every Classroom* is due entirely to the discovery by teachers in every classroom that magazines are good for learning and good for teaching. As the newspaper, magazines are in constant use because students will learn from them and teachers can teach from them. No higher recommendation is possible for any textbook.

THE SCHOOL LIBRARY

A Philosophy of Use

The concept of the school library requires the same sort of basic reconsideration that this program advocates for the teaching of reading and writing. Many observers have remarked the depressing lack of visual appeal and the even more depressing lack of reading activity in public school libraries. Most depressing of all, however, are the schools so overcrowded that they have little or no room for a library. The following recommendations are particularly aimed at alleviating these three problems of space, visual appeal, and reading activity:

Where change is most badly needed is in unexamined ideas of economy which seem to dictate types of books and methods of display. For what reason other than economy of space are books displayed with their spines out? The spine of a book with Dewey Decimal notations upon it is no more attractive than any other spine with such markings would be. And yet we expect the partially literate child, who relates through words to very little, to relate to books through words printed on their spines. This is the same child, however, whom we know to be attracted to pictures ranging from those in comic books to those on the television screen. Why then do we not make the most of his tastes and predispositions, give up the false economy which shelves efficient numbers of unread books, and attract him to books through the bright pictures on their covers? Let us replace the typically drab, unread books of our school libraries—libraries full of books with covers unpictured and unopened—with paperbound books that attract children (just as they attract adults) by means of the pictured covers that experienced commercial artists and advertising men have made inviting.

Clearly I am not speaking of a traditional library arrangement when I refer to book covers rather than book spines on display. School librarians should take a useful lesson from operators of paperbound bookstores, who have learned to let their merchandise sell itself by arranging their stores so that the customer is surrounded by colorful and highly descriptive paper covers. But what of the expense of purchasing paperbound books to begin with, and of maintaining a steady supply to replace the easily tattered, broken, and lost paperback? What of the expense? Two questions must be asked in return: What is more expensive than the waste of human intellect implied in a library of unread books? And what sort of destruction is more admirable than the book tattered and finally broken beyond repair by the hands of eager readers? We have been too long without such destruction; the time has come for our school libraries to invite it.

If reading activity follows visual appeal as effect follows cause, what about space problems of shelving books with their covers showing? The answer lies in the wall racks and free-standing spinners traditionally used to promote paperback sales in corner drugstores and other places where space is at a premium. The problem of library space has also another interesting possibility of solution—the combination classroom and library advocated by this program. In order for the library to become an organic part of the English curriculum, it should be available as a classroom to all teachers and should be specified as the place of meeting once each week for every English class. Where no room is readily available, as is so often the case in the old and seriously overcrowded buildings where the disadvantaged child finds his education, a larger classroom can often be easily adapted to the minimal space requirements of revolving wire racks full of paperbound books.

A third alternative to the formal school library or the classroom library has recently been made available by book distributors in some areas of the United States and, I am told, would be made available in many more if requested by school officials. This alternative can be employed by itself or, far better, it can be a very useful complement to the school's own holdings. I am referring here to the mo-

42

bile bookstore, a trailer purchased by the local book distributor at his own expense and stocked by him with titles suggested by a committee of teachers from the local public and parochial schools. Yes, commercialism certainly does rear its thick wallet here, for the books are *sold* to students, with school and distributor sharing in the small profits. Mobile bookrooms will make neither school nor distributor wealthy, but they do represent an ideal instance of identity of interest in the public and private sectors of our economy. Schools must train greater numbers of more willing readers in order to justify their very existence; book distributors (and publishers) must create more readers in order to survive. One book purchased from a mobile bookstore by one reluctant reader represents a significant double accomplishment for education and industry alike. Educators simply cannot afford the luxury of ignoring the products and the knowledge of the commercial world. The very idea of an inviolate "school world" is worse than indefensible; it is damaging in the extreme to the very concept it seeks to perpetuate and protect.

Fundamental to the malaise from which conventional school libraries suffer is the universal assumption that students will use them because they are there. Were this assumption applied to other human activities, ranging from toilet-training to tool-using, only catastrophe could be the result. Regarding the library as something less than an irresistible attraction is a very useful first step in revitalizing it. Implicit in this approach is a review of its lending procedures. Instead of placing the responsibility for first (and, too often, last) acquaintance upon the student and/or the teacher, the responsibility should be put where it rightfully belongs—upon the books themselves. *Give* each child a paperbound book or two to begin his school year. Let him understand that he may have any other paperbound book in the library by the simple expedient of trading a book he has for a book he wants. Then *schedule* him twice each week for the opportunity of book borrowing, and if our experience at the Maxey School has been any guide—stand back and enjoy the sight of children reading.

Selecting the Books

Just what selection procedures create the best paperback library? Impersonal statistics combined with personal knowledge can often be confusing and misleading. For example—the youngest boy at BTS is twelve, the oldest eighteen; the average boy reads as well as a fourth grader, and most are in junior high before they come to the Maxey School. Almost all have lived materially disadvantaged lives; almost all have come from culturally impoverished worlds. At the age of twelve they know more about physical man—from sex of some kinds to violence of all kinds —than any child should and most adults ever will. At the age of eighteen they know less about the world outside the neighborhoods in which they have lived (all alike; moving often is easier than paying the rent) than middle class children half their age. Everybody knows about them. But who knows them? And who knows what kind of books they will read?

Haunted by the spectre of our own ignorance, we took refuge in a copy of the 1964 *Paperbound Books In Print*. We tore the title list into six equal sections, one section for each English teacher. In this section, each teacher placed a check beside each book he thought the boys would like to read, and two checks beside each book he thought the boys would like to read and he would like to teach. Then he exchanged sections with another teacher and, using crosses instead of checks, did the same with the section he received. Next, each teacher found a section he hadn't yet read and no third reader had marked; this section he marked with small circles in the same way. Finally, each teacher took the last section in his possession, made a list of the books with three different kinds of marks beside them, and checked the ones that had at least one of those marks twice. When the last step had been performed, we had our library list. In addition, we had a list of books the teachers would like to have in class-size sets for teaching purposes.

Now for appeal to the final authority—the boys. But

first the books had to be obtained with a return privilege. We knew that our list was intelligent, democratic, inclusive, unique. What we didn't know was whether it contained books the boys would read. If we spent the little money we had on books that would go unread, we might just as well have stocked our school library with all the customary hardbound books that nobody ever reads anyway and saved ourselves a good deal of trouble. Out of our need came one of the best experiences we were to have at the Maxey School. We discovered the wise charity of Ivan Ludington, Sr., and his Ludington News Company of Detroit.

The letter I wrote was something less than a masterpiece. Only college presidents and skid-row bums are really good at begging. But the answer I got would have made a president proud and a bum delirious. Two days after I mailed the letter the phone in my office rang. Ivan Ludington speaking—what did I need and where did I need it? He would be glad to come to Ann Arbor to make arrangements. No, I would come to Detroit. Somehow that seemed to be the least I could do. It was. It was also the most I could do. At the time I write this, Mr. Ludington has been supplying the school for more than a year with all the paperbound books and magazines we request—absolutely free of any charge. Thus far the numbers are something like 4000 paperbacks and 10,000 magazines. Combine these figures with the equally remarkable generosity of that excellent paper, *The Detroit News* (one hundred copies a day, seven days a week), and the principle of saturation begins to take on a clearer meaning.

When I spoke of the "wise charity" of Ivan Ludington, I was referring to his ancient and honorable idea that what a man gives is often what a man gets. An established distributor of books and magazines, one who has thoroughly covered his territory, has only two hopes for increasing his business: One is that those who read will read more; or, to put it another way, that those who read will reproduce their kind in increasing numbers. The distributor's second hope is that those who do not read will begin to read, and that they will produce children who read. Demographical-

45

ly speaking, these hopes are highly unreliable. Not only do both groups—readers and non-readers alike—tend to reproduce themselves, but the non-readers (grouped statistically at the lower end of the socio-economic scale) outproduce the readers in significant numbers. I know of no more dramatic illustration of this than the private circulation figures of a very important metropolitan daily newspaper. Recently I was told that the paper's percentage of the market had dropped significantly in recent years, even though the number of its readers had continued to rise. Equally interesting, its chief rival was experiencing the same phenomenon. That information should surprise no one. As the higher birthrate of the lower classes increases the percentage of those classes in the total population, a lesser percentage of the total population can be identified as willing readers. We are, in short, becoming inexorably a nation of non-readers.

As teachers and parents we are desperately concerned for the intellectual welfare of the children of today who become the statistics of tomorrow. But before we believe that our inclination and training automatically qualify us to prescribe remedies for the growing sickness of unwilling minds, we should tell ourselves how much our very education disqualifies us as experts in the mental life of disadvantaged and impoverished children. Those of us who participated in selecting the original twelve hundred titles for the Maxey paperback library will never again have to be reminded of how little we know about the students we teach. None of us will forget the untouched seven hundred titles that decorated our gleaming drugstore spinners while the boys read and reread the five hundred they liked.

My private prediction for our list was that some two hundred books might go unread, largely because they seemed to me to be either too difficult or too passive for a sixteen-year-old boy with a ninety IQ who reads at a fourth grade level. But I had no doubts whatsoever that the remaining thousand were books the boys would read if we could display them attractively within an effective language program. I could hardly have been more mistaken. Not only was I one hundred percent wrong in my estimate of the number of successful books on our list, but seventy-five of the books I had thought would be ignored proved to be popular with the boys. The five hundred winners of our book derby are listed alphabetically by author in the *Reading List* at the end of this book. The only place we can be *certain* they will be read is at the Maxey School. They have been read for the past year, and they have been attractive enough to raise the average book use in the school to more than two books per week for each boy. A very few boys still read nothing, and equally few read a book a day. Between these extremes, we have a great many boys who read book after book because they like the books they are reading. Which is only another way of saying that they *like to read.*

The Reading List: An Analysis

Warming up the cold list of five hundred are the sparks of light and heat given off by rubbing boys against books. Moments like this, for instance: Monday morning, just before the first class of the week, an English teacher is about to close the door to his room as a seventeen year old runs past to a classroom further down the hall. The boy turns, pulls out of his shirt Dick Gregory's book, *From the Back of the Bus,* waves it at the teacher, and shouts while already turning away, "I bought it, man, I bought it! Bought four more while I was home. Didn't steal none!" Bought or stolen, those five books were the first books that boy had ever owned. Home for a weekend as part of the school's rehabilitation program, he had been able to think of no better use for his time and money than to spend both on paperback books from the corner drugstore. Even if he had stolen them, this was certainly the first time he had stolen *books.*

Or the Case of the Bonds going out of Stock: The boys wanted the James Bond books. What's more, they wanted them loudly and often. Our usual response to their desire to read books we didn't have was considerably tempered by the covers of the Ian Fleming novels and by our limited knowledge of what went on between those covers. Most

47

of us had seen *Goldfinger,* but few of us had read any of Bond's adventures. My own response had been to suspect the usual book-movie relationship, i.e., if Pussy Galore was a character in the *movie,* how much radical cleansing had the producer done in order to make the author's work acceptable on the screen? That suspicion, plus the undressed covers, had kept the Bond books out of our library.

Like all other censors, whether self-appointed or otherwise, I was insufficient to the job. When it occurred to me —as the howl for Bond grew—that I might at least read the books I was banning, I read them all as a kind of penance. I was embarrassed by their contents; I was embarrassed by the discovery, for instance, that *Goldfinger* is far sexier to see than to read, and that Ian Fleming was as proper a Britisher as ever ogled young ladies from a club window. Henry Miller at the age of ten could have spotted Fleming-Bond two red lights and three double-beds, and won the race in a crawl. We ordered a dozen copies of every book.

The books were delivered to the librarian one morning just as she was going out into the hall to help another teacher separate a couple of featherweight battlers. Ten boys from the same class were in the library at the time. The bell for change of class had just rung, and they were at the door, preparing to leave, when the teacher with them told them to remain inside the library until the fight in the hall was under control. Then he joined the librarian and the boys were left momentarily alone in the library. The librarian says she was gone long enough to walk fifteen feet from her door, see that the situation needed a man, and turn back to get the male teacher who had been in the library with his class. When she saw him coming, she returned immediately to the library. She could not, she is sure, have been gone more than three minutes. As she entered the library, the ten boys were leaving by the other door to go to their next class. She called to the last one to shut the door. She remembers how he jumped when she called his name.

Not until half-an-hour later, when she began to catalogue

the Bond books, did she realize why he had been so startled. In the brief minutes she had been out of the room, eighty of the 007 adventure stories had disappeared. A brief survey followed by a little arithmetic led her to the realization that each boy had taken one complete set of the eight titles she had received. Though impressed by such a feat of distribution, and pleased by so evident and massive a desire to read, she felt she could do no less than, at the very least, catalogue the books before they were stolen. When she entered their classroom, the boys were upset only because she had discovered the larceny so soon. Nobody had gotten to do any reading. Leaving questions of crime and punishment to philosophers and psychologists, the librarian promised the boys they could each borrow two of Fleming's books if they'd come in at the end of the day when she had them catalogued. Her final comment was that she had made the promise because their disappointment was so real. They had taken the books because they wanted to read them.

James Bond is a fitting introduction to our five hundred. Roughly two-thirds of the list is divided almost equally into six categories, five of which are tailored to the taste of a Bond buff. In descending order, these five categories are War Stories, Tales of Suspense and Horror, Sports Stories, Tales of Adventure, and Science Fiction/Space Science. War Stories claim about 12% of the list, while 9% of the books is devoted to the category of Science Fiction/Space Science. Between these two are the Tales of Suspense and Horror, Sports Stories, and Tales of Adventure, each amounting to between 10 and 11% of the titles in the library.

Though our library has more War Stories than any other kind, they are not the most popular of our books. That distinction is reserved for the sixth category, comprising about 50 titles or 10% of the list. These are books exclusively by or about Negroes, and they are read many times more often than the War Stories which are their nearest competitors. This phenomenon has several possible explanations—the Negro population at the Maxey School, which fluctuates between 40 and 60%; the climate of racial concern in the

United States—but its probable explanation seems to me to owe at least as much to the quality of books by authors like James Baldwin and Richard Wright, our most popular writers, and John Howard Griffin, author of our most popular book, *Black Like Me*. The books these men write each contain a cry from the heart that black and white alike can hear and respond to. We have tried to discriminate our readers and we have failed. Books by and about Negroes are read equally at the Maxey School by White and Negro children alike.

The popularity of books by writers like Baldwin, Griffin, and Wright was no surprise to anyone, but the continued currency of the War Stories was less expected. Certainly the war in Vietnam has done nothing to depress the market, but the boys' interest in such stories seems to be older, deeper, and more generalized than the history of any particular war. A boy who begins with Commander Beach's *Run Silent, Run Deep* is likely to go on to Beach's *Submarine* and Frank Bonham's *War Beneath the Sea*. Such quasi-sequential reading is encouraged by our display racks in which we group all books likely to cater to the same taste. Thus Patrick Reid's *Escape from Colditz* customarily takes the interested reader to Eric Williams' masterpiece, *The Tunnel Escape* (or, as many of us knew it before, *The Tunnel*). In the same way, one book by Quentin Reynolds is likely to lead to another, as do the various War and Combat books edited by Don Congdon.

Only somewhat less patronized than the rack of War Stories are those racks filled with Tales of Suspense and Horror and Tales of Adventure. Leading the former group are books edited by Rod Serling, with his three collections of stories from the Twilight Zone pacing the field. Also popular are the various groups of Alfred Hitchcock's favorite tales, especially *Stories My Mother Never Told Me*. The teenage rage for monsters has improved the currency of such old favorites as Mary Shelley's *Frankenstein* and Victor Hugo's *The Hunchback of Notre Dame*, as well as accounting for the popularity of Boris Karloff's *Favorite Horror Stories*. Equally well read are the Tales of Adventure, with the boys making little if any difference amongst a variety of story-tellers from other eras such as Sax Rohmer, Rudyard Kipling, Jules Verne, Herman Melville, and James Fenimore Cooper, and an equal variety from their own era such as Charles Nordhoff and James Norman Hall, Ernest Gann, and Patrick O'Connor. The Fu Manchu books keep company with *The Pathfinder, Billy Budd,* and *Journey to the Center of the Earth. Fate Is the Hunter* and *The Black Tiger* are in constant use.

Sports Stories and Science Fiction/Space Science, the two categories which complete the six most largely represented in the Maxey library, differ from each other more widely than any of the other book groupings. The quality of the writing in the Sport Stories varies from mediocre to embarrassing, while paperbacks of Science Fiction are generally the best written books in the library. Science Fiction got quite a play when our library first opened, with authors like Isaac Asimov, Ray Bradbury, Robert Heinlein, and Andre Norton, and editors such as J. W. Campbell and Groff Conklin having their stories and collections often read. But the best Science Fiction is a kind of intellectual ballet, and our boys dance the monkey, the jerk, and the frug. As Asimov, Bradbury, and Heinlein declined, Norton's star rose. Specializing as she does in simple action rather than complex imagination, Norton's adventures were read while far better writers languished. Today, Science Fiction is the least read of the major book categories in our library.

One of the most interesting facts we have gleaned from observing boys and their books at Maxey is the relative unpopularity of imagined Sports Stories and Westerns. Recalling my own adolescent reading habits, a staple of my diet was the shoeless boy from the mountains who just happened to be driving a baseball five hundred feet (a baseball served-up by his daddy who was a former minor-league pitcher) when a major league scout came looking for a jug of mountain dew. And I knew personally every fast gun in the West. But not our boys. They are far more interested in the story of Yogi Berra or Floyd Patterson than they are in the accomplishments of the greatest imaginary hero, and the rate at which they read Westerns would turn Zane grey.

Westerns form one of the seven minor categories amongst which approximately a third of our library books are more or less evenly divided. The other six groups are Detective Stories, Animal and Nature Stories, Books of Humor, Facts-of-Life and Self-Improvement Books, History and Non-Sports Biography, and Car Books. These six categories each have anywhere from five to three percent of the books in the library, but they receive nothing like equal patronage. Two unequal groups are readily formed, with the first including the more popular detective, humor, car, and facts-of-life books, while the second is composed of the less read animal and nature stories together with history and non-sports biography. Detective stories get the biggest play of all, with the incomparable James Bond making readers galore. Without Bond and the two Mikes, Hammer and Shane, the category would languish, for deducing detectives are not swinging detectives in the eyes of our teenage boys, and neither Agatha Christie nor Erle Stanley Gardner has been able to cut it at Maxey.

We have all been interested to see how much action the Facts-of-Life and Self-Improvement Books have gotten. Of course the implication of sex in any title guarantees that book an audience. One of the funniest and most meaningful tangents of this blanket guarantee at Maxey involved *The Scarlet Letter*: On a Friday morning, an English teacher watched one of his poorest readers choose Hawthorne's novel from the rack. Knowing how difficult the boy would find the book, and fearing that he would be discouraged by the experience, the teacher suggested that perhaps he had chosen *The Scarlet Letter* thinking it was something else. "Ain't this the one about a whore?" asked the boy. "And don't that big A stand for whore?" When the teacher had to admit that this description was more or less correct, the boy had heard enough. If it was a book about a whore, it was the book for him.

Three days later, on Monday, the same boy came to his English teacher with *The Scarlet Letter* in hand and two sheets of notebook paper. On those two sheets, front and back, were all the words—and their definitions—the boy hadn't known in the first eleven pages of the book. He had clearly spent the weekend with Hawthorne and the dictionary, and he was looking for praise—which he got, lavishly. His English teacher was amazed: the two sheets of notebook paper represented at least six hours work. According to the teacher, this was a boy who may not have spent six hours reading since he was twelve years old, and who had no apparent idea of how to use a dictionary when he came to the Maxey School. Motivated by Hawthorne's whore, he fought his way through the book. He produced no more lists, but he kept at the book (while reading other novels) for an entire month, and for that month and longer his conversations with his English teacher were full of his view of what was happening to Hester Prynne. Proceeding as slowly as he did through the story of her life, she took on dimensions of reality for him which authors dream of imparting to their readers and teachers despair of conveying to their students.

One implication of this boy's experience is especially interesting: Hawthorne's vocabulary is difficult for *college* students. I have taught *The Scarlet Letter* to freshmen and sophomores at two universities where better than half the students come from the top ten percent of their high school class. Each of the half-dozen times I have taught it, I have followed the first reading assignment of the introductory chapter, "The Custom House," with a ten-minute written quiz asking for definitions of ten words chosen from the first three pages of that chapter. Each time I made the assignment in terms of "read the introductory chapter *carefully*." Every student was allowed to use his textbook and any notes he may have prepared. Only the dictionary was forbidden. Full credit was given for the barest suggestion of knowledge, e.g., "bark: some kind of boat"; "truculency: meanness;" even for "prolix: says a lot." But no matter how ominously I emphasized the word "carefully" in the assignment, and no matter how undemanding my standards of definition, no more than one-fifth of any of the six classes managed to define as many as five of the ten words.

My ringing, rhetorical, unfair question as I return the

quizzes at the next meeting of those unfortunate classes is always, "How can you claim to have *read* anything when you don't even know what the words mean?" The question is unfair because in spite of appearances, I do not much care that they can not define the words. For I know perfectly well that they can read with great understanding without knowing what all the words mean. The quiz is merely one method of forcing a slower and more careful reading practice upon students convinced that fast reading is the best reading. The quality of their good understanding invariably comes to light during the discussions that follow the ten-minute quizzes.

But what has this to do with a juvenile delinquent struggling through *The Scarlet Letter?* Just this: Semi-literate readers do not need semi-literate books. The simplistic language of much of the life-leeched literature inflicted upon the average schoolchild is not even justifiable in its own terms. Bright, average, dull—whatever the classification of the child's intellect, he is immeasurably better off with books that are too difficult for him than books that are too easy. But that involves a whole theory of education. All I mean to emphasize here is what teachers have observed at both the Maxey and Garnet-Patterson schools and I have experienced as a teacher of considerably different students: "Reading" is a peculiarly personal interaction between the child and the book, an interaction as different in each case as readers may differ from each other in breadth of experience and quality of mind. But *in no case* does this interaction demand an understanding of every word by the reader. In fact, the threshold of understanding—of meaningful interaction—is surprisingly low and can be pleasurably crossed in many complex books by many simple readers.

Just as Hester Prynne's affair with the Rev. Dimmesdale gives *The Scarlet Letter* a consistent currency in our library, so do the titles of books like Maxine Davis' *Sex and the Adolescent,* Evelyn Duvall's *Facts of Life and Love for Teenagers* and *The Art of Dating,* Havelock Ellis' *On Life and Sex,* and Aaron Krich's *Facts of Love and Marriage for Young People.* All are well used at Maxey, as are the books where the author's name is more important than the title—Dick Clark's two books, *To Goof or Not to Goof* and *Your Happiest Years,* and *Ann Landers Talks to Teens.* Of surprising popularity in this same category are Carolyn Coggins' *Book of Etiquette and Manners* and Jack Heise's *The Painless Way to Stop Smoking.*

Advice on how to date, make love, and get married— not necessarily in that order—is more sought after than other how-to information, but other subsections of the category claim a substantial readership. The two largest groups of titles here are the sport and the language books; rather unexpectedly one set is about as well-read as the other. In the former group are paperbacks like Red Auerback's *Basketball,* Herman Masin's series of books on *How to Star in Basketball, How to Star in Baseball,* and *How to Star in Football,* Harold O'Connor's *How to Star in Track and Field,* and Albert Morehead's *The Official Rules of Card Games.* In the latter group are books primarily aimed at vocabulary and spelling, such as Wilfred Funk's *Thirty Days to a More Powerful Vocabulary,* Ruth Gleeson's *Words Most Often Misspelled and Mispronounced,* Roger Goodman's *New Ways to Greater Word Power,* Frances Hall's *20 Steps to Perfect Spelling,* Norman Lewis' *Rapid Vocabulary Builder,* and Harry Maddox on *How to Study.* It should be said, however, that all of these together are somewhat less popular than Fred Horsley's *The Hot Rod Handbook.*

Fred Horsley brings us to a type of book which is limited in number but virtually unlimited in attraction. In BTS language, it's the hogbook. You know, man—the hog, the bomb, the sheen. Man, you know—you get your vines and your boats from outa your fox's crib and you ease into your hog to slide off and kick some grips. You're gonna jack up that man on account of he took your slat but he didn't bring you no pluck to get your head bad.—Hogs, bombs, sheens; cars by any other name ride just as sweet. Vines are clothes, boats are shoes, you fox is your girl, and a crib is a pad—er, a house. When I kick some grips or I pack you up, you better slide, man (go away quick), because I'm going to fight you. And for a mighty good reason: You took my money (slat) but you didn't deliver the wine (pluck) to get me drunk (get my head bad). So there's nothing left for me to do but break out my pack, blow pot, and listen to this here bad jam until I cop some Z's. Ain't this about a willie? (. . . open my package of marijuana cigarettes, smoke one, and listen to this good record until I fall asleep. But I tell you, I can't believe this is happening to *me*!)

Undisputed king of the sheens is Henry Gregor Felsen with his *Hot Rod, Street Rod, Crash Club,* and *Road Rocket*. William Campbell Gault hits on all eight with *Drag Strip* and *Speedway Challenge,* as does Philip Harkins in *The Day of the Drag Race* and *Road Race*. R. W. Campbell employs the magic formula, combining hogs and girls in his *Drag Doll*. Evan Jones edits the popular *High Gear,* a collection of stories by authors like Steinbeck, Thurber, Mauldin, and Saroyan who write about fast cars and their drivers. Ken Purdy, "the man who knows more about the great cars than anyone else in America," writes about them in *The Kings of the Road*. And he writes about them so well that Dusenbergs, Bugattis, and Mercedes are as familiar to hog buffs as A-Bones, Beasts, and Mother-Heads. What, man! You don't know the difference between an iron that's been frenched, chopped, and channelled, and a gasser that's been bull-nosed? It's alright, man, neither do I.

At about the same time during their year at Maxey, most boys are likely to read their way through the ten titles which form the heart of the Humor section of the library. The time is generally soon after their arrival, just after they've been introduced to the library and just before they've encompassed the idea that the library is a source of pleasure rather than of pain. During that crucial transition period, picture-books with familiar characters are ports in a storm of change; Dennis the Menace and Charley Brown are welcomed with smiles of anxious relief. Boy after boy reads quickly through Hank Ketchum's six titles and Charley Schulz's four before he pushes himself into the deeper water of words without pictures.

After such a categorical examination of the list of five

hundred, perhaps a few general facts will be welcome: Both the average and the mean retail price of the books in the Maxey library is fifty cents. No book is priced higher than ninety-five cents, only twelve percent cost more than sixty cents, and only three percent cost more than seventy-five cents. Customary school discount actually reduces the cost of the average book on our reading list to about forty cents, a price which must surely be the biggest educational bargain since the invention of the underpaid teacher.

The books contained in this list and cited in the preceding discussion are recommended neither as the best nor the only ones of their kind. Why, for instance, do we have one of Irving Shulman's books—*West Side Story*—and not others like *Cry Tough* and *The Amboy Dukes?* Or what criteria did we use to eliminate *Doctor No* and *From Russia With Love* in our choice of Ian Fleming's 007 adventures? And what happened to Evelyn Duvall's book on *Sense and Nonsense About Sex?* Why *An American Tragedy* and not *Sister Carrie?* How did we manage to include *From the Back of the Bus* and omit *Nigger,* Dick Gregory's other book? All of these questions generally have one of two answers—either no teacher recommended them (as in *Cry Tough* or *The Amboy Dukes* or *Sister Carrie*) or the Ludington News Company, which has given us all our paperbacks, did not have them in stock (*Doctor No* and *From Russia With Love*) when we picked up that section of our order. Only one book is not accounted for by these two answers—*Nigger.* It is not found in our library because the title is offensive to some of our teachers and students. Gregory himself makes the best possible comment on that kind of censorship when he writes his dedication: "Dear Momma—Wherever you are, if ever you hear the word 'nigger' again, remember they are advertising my book."

A GUIDE FOR TEACHERS IN
AREAS OTHER THAN ENGLISH AND
SOCIAL STUDIES

The program in reading and writing which has been developed in the Maxey School and is now being instituted in the District of Columbia public schools depends partially upon you, the instructor whose professional competence lies outside the area customarily defined as "English." Making an English program in any degree dependent upon teachers in other subject areas may at first seem unusual and unlikely to succeed—after all, what do *you* know about teaching English?—but a second look demonstrates that the program is only unusual. In its dependence upon teachers of other subjects, it is likely to succeed for at least two very good reasons: because all teachers care enough about their own students and enough about their own subjects to recognize the potential benefits to both of willing competence in English throughout the student body.

We are all familiar with the complaint that teaching partially literate children *anything* is difficult because they can neither sufficiently understand oral directions nor adequately interpret written instructions. Though the complaint is often repeated, it has never been directly answered; instead, it has been referred again and again to the English teacher, the one person with the least chance of finding the answer. He has the least chance of satisfying the complaint precisely because he is the English teacher, instructor in the one classroom in which the partially literate child has always experienced his worst failures. Given much help by his colleagues, the English teacher may be able to help the non-literate child. By himself, however, he has amply demonstrated that he cannot do enough. The purpose of this plan, therefore, is to help the English teacher to help the student. In so doing, every teacher will

58

be helping each child to be a better student in the teacher's own subject area.

The basic assumption upon which this program is built is the non-literate child's desperate need for more language competence than he has. The child who cannot understand oral and written directions becomes the adult who cannot hold any job above the level of the simplest manual labor or household drudgery; in a technocracy characterized by decreasing individual labor, such jobs become more and more difficult to find. Furthermore, and equally important, partially literate children cannot depend upon the language they cannot use; they must depend upon other means of expression—force, for example—which they are sure they can use. Perhaps if we can give them language, they can give up some of the wordless violence which they use as their megaphone to communicate with a world which they cannot reach in any other way.

Too much emphasis cannot be placed upon the claim that making all instructors in the school teachers of English must be profitable to all subjects in the curriculum. What subject, after all, does not depend upon language for its teaching and for its learning? In what subject would both teacher and student not be greatly helped if they could understand each other's conversation and if the student could be relied upon to comprehend written directions? The answer of course is that no subject is independent of language; the obvious conclusion, therefore, is that all subjects should participate in teaching what all depend upon for their existence.

The role of the teacher in subject areas other than English is clear, for minimal demands of the program are remarkably simple; its maximal possibilities are unknown and lie entirely in the individual teacher's hands. This approach to teaching and learning has no absolute precedents, no irrevocable traditions, and no unchallengeable methods; the methods it advocates are easily encompassed in the following summary:

I Reading

A. Use of popular magazines and newspapers

1. Part of the attempt to create a new learning environment for partially literate children is the use of reading materials more or less familiar to them as part of the non-school world in which learning—especially language learning—was never forced upon them. Since popular magazines and newspapers are not part of the school world as they know it, such materials greatly recommend themselves for use in this approach.

2. In addition to the aspect of novelty which such texts possess, they have another and more important justification: they are easy to handle and easy to read. Each teacher should plan part of his teaching effort around newspapers and magazines; within them is contained matter which is relevant to every course in the curriculum.

B. Use of paperbound books

1. Part of the effort of English teachers to make reading more enjoyable for their students will be very extensive use of paperbound books in their teaching procedures and availability of such books throughout the school. Since other courses may not be primarily reading courses, other teachers cannot be expected to use these books in the same manner. Instead, the program asks that all teachers carefully research the materials in their disciplines in the effort to discover and use any paperbound books and magazines having special application to their subject area.

2. The library created as a result of and as an aid to this program is built upon the model of a paperbound bookstore. It is designed to make a wide selection of easily handled, attractively covered books available to the student on a barter basis. If these are books that the student will read with pleasure, then they become a vehicle to promote learning with an ease seldom found in other texts.

Recognizing this, teachers in subject areas other than English should thoroughly explore possibilities of using the library and of suggesting additions to its collection which will benefit their own teaching.

C. Use of written directions

1. The third aspect of this reading program in classrooms outside of English is careful use of written directives. One probable assumption of learning to read is that people very often learn to read when they have to. Or to put it another way, when reading seems necessary to survival, then it becomes a process to master rather than an intrusion to resist. Few students ever really cared whether Jack went up the hill or Jill fell down, but all of them care to accomplish something somebody else will praise, even if that somebody else is a teacher. If the road to accomplishment is paved with written directions, and that road is made neither too long nor too difficult, a student may see pleasure itself as reason enough for traveling it.

II Writing

A. Scheduled writing in the classroom

1. Just as no one ever learned to read except by reading, certainly no one ever learned to write except by writing. Making the act of writing a normative, inescapable part of the child's school environment is one of the chief aims of this plan. One thing we are certain of: The average public school student has always been able to identify writing as a part of "English" and therefore avoidable because the English class was the only one in which writing played any noticeable role. Changing this attitude is crucial to increasing the child's ability to write.

Making the act of writing a standard part of every classroom assumes that each teacher will follow a standard plan. In this case, the plan requires that every teacher in every humanities and sciences classroom collect five *in-class* writing assignments from each student during each two-week period of the course. This plan neither prescribes nor is vitally concerned with the length or content of these papers. It assumes that the repetitive act of writing is the only essential element, and prefers to count papers rather than words. It also realizes, however, that the process of making writing an unavoidable part of classes in which writing has been unimportant before may at first be difficult for teachers newly involved. Therefore, the plan is based upon small groups centered about an English teacher whose responsibility will be to make the new program as easy as possible for the teachers in his group and as profitable as possible for the students.

In addition to acting as a consultant to his colleagues, the English teacher will also handle one of the five sets of papers received bi-weekly by each teacher in his group. The two remaining weekly paper sets should be handled by the subject instructor himself. One should be read for content; the other should be filed *unread* in the student's folder. This latter action, unusual in any system of education, is based upon the analogy of exercise: Just as the music teacher does not listen to all the exercises of the music student, so should the writing teacher not read all the exercises of the writing student. This method allows the student to get the practice he needs without at the same time overburdening the teacher.

B. Unscheduled writing in the classroom.

This sort of writing practice should be a natural outgrowth of learning procedures within the classroom and a natural complement to planned written exercises. Implementation will require improvisation on the part of the teacher. When a student requires a new tool, or asks a complex question, the teacher's reaction should be to ask for the request or the question in writing, just as the child's superior may do in the world of daily employment outside of and beyond public school.

Note: To teachers of industrial arts, home economics, music, and art—student writing is very much less a natural part of your teaching method than some of the other subjects in the curriculum. This new program in English will find a different place in each of your classes. To begin with, it merely asks your tolerant support of an effort that touches each of us as teachers—an effort to bring language competence to children who need it as badly as they need good food and steady affection.

THE ENGLISH CLASSROOM

Imagine the scene: Eleven delinquent boys sitting in an English classroom, each reading intensely in his own copy of the same paperbound book. *Goldfinger? Black Like Me? West Side Story?* What else could generate such attention from a group like that? A dictionary.

Breast, whore, lesbian, prostitute, vagina, copulation, intercourse, etc. etc. etc.—the boys find them all. The dictionary is any fifty-cent paperbound lexicon; after a few days of use it opens automatically to a page with one of the "good" words on it. A boy raises his head to ask of nobody, "How you spell that U-word?"

"What word?"

"You know, man. That good word."

"You mean U-terrace?"

"Yeah. Whats a U-terrace?"

"At's where you makes a U-turn."

"Oh man you *so* dumb!"

Whatever the original attraction, the dictionary has rivaled the success of the journal in the English program at Maxey and has been transplanted into the public schools with equal vigor. The unavoidable conclusion is that children *like* dictionaries when dictionaries are part of a program designed to make language pleasurable as well as useful.

When a student first enters either the public or penal school, he is given—amongst other things—a paperbound dictionary. He is told that the dictionary is his, that it won't be collected or replaced by the school, and that he can carry it with him or he can leave it at home or in his room or anywhere else that pleases him. If he chooses to carry his dictionary with him, he will be able to use it in class—any class. If he does not have his own dictionary available, he will find a set of paperbound dictionaries in every one of his classrooms. These sets range from class-size in

English and Social Studies classes to smaller numbers in classrooms where the dictionary is less crucial to the subject. They are, according to the teachers, in constant *voluntary* use.

Our expectation at the training school had been that the dictionaries, if successful, would be transported constantly back and forth between the school and the boys' rooms. As one result of that expectation, paperbound dictionaries were ordered for each student's personal use, but only one or two desk dictionaries were ordered for each classroom. Our mistake was quickly apparent: The boys wanted to use their dictionaries but they also wanted to keep them as part of their permanent possessions, safe in their own rooms. Experimentally and tentatively, we obtained paperbound dictionaries in class-size sets for each English teacher. Almost immediately we began to hear from teachers of other subjects: Why were they left out? The dictionary was as useful to them as it was to the English teacher. How about sets for their rooms? Happily, we purchased more books; now, all over the school, dictionaries are in use. Teachers of all subjects have discovered that an interest in words often becomes an interest in the ideas the words convey.

With the experience at Maxey as our pattern, we ordered individual books and class-size sets for every child and every classroom in the public school. The dictionaries were an immediate and resounding success. In one of her periodic progress reports, Mrs. Thelma Jones, Chairman of the English Department, told the story of the boy who used the word "damn" in class. "That'll be enough of that swearing," said his teacher.

"Enough of *what?*" asked the boy.

Refusing to be baited, the teacher turned her attention elsewhere, but not before she caught a glimpse of a peculiar expression on the boy's face followed by some activity at his seat. She had all but forgotten about him when his excited voice broke through the classroom conversation: "Swearing—that's cussing! The dictionary says so!" He hadn't understood the teacher, but he had possessed the

65

means to arrive at understanding. No learning experience can be better than that.

Though the dictionary appears to be equally successful at both schools, the pattern of its usage differs in one important respect—mobility. Where the protective sense of possession inhibits movement of the dictionary from bedroom to classroom at the Maxey School, the sense of pride in possession seems to have the opposite effect in public school. Many of the children are proud of their very own dictionary; as a result, they carry and use it with a pleasure usually reserved for objects more familiar than wordbooks.

The dictionary is a convenient introduction to the practice of the English classroom because it has universal application within the curriculum of any school. "The English Classroom" is the title of the *last* chapter in this essay because one of the primary concerns of the program called *English In Every Classroom* is to place the teaching of English in a context within which it can succeed. The reason for this preoccupation is the conviction that English is unique in its dependence upon other subjects for depth and reinforcement. An English class which does not draw some of its materials from other subjects, and which cannot make its influence felt in those same subjects, is as moribund as Latin grammar in the public schools, and might just as well be a class in Latin as in English. Given the proper surroundings—seeing a reflection of itself in all courses, even as it reflects them—the English class can be the meaningful focus of the student's education. Placed in a context where reading and writing are as necessary and inevitable as nourishment and sleep, the student, the course, and the instructor will thrive together.

Of first importance must be definition of the general purpose of the English class. This purpose must not be defined once again in the usual impersonal and exalted professional terms; it must not be defined in the customary platitudes about improving the moral nature and verbal performance of the child through exposing him to the good and the great in literature. Instead, it must be expressed against the restrictive reality of the students' previous experience. Far better no English class at all than one dedicated primarily to making reasonably respectable spellers and grammarians. Surely the *ultimate* goal of the English teacher must be the making of humanists who are competent readers and writers; furthermore, this training must include competence in grammar and spelling. But, just as surely, the English classroom should be the place in which a learning experience of far greater importance than instruction in the mechanics of language takes place. To the means of effecting that end, the following recommendations are made for the philosophy and conduct of the English class:

(1) *That the approach to literature be social rather than literary.*

This recommendation is based upon a pedagogical philosophy which finds "He give me the Buk" a more desirable statement than "He gave me the book," if the former reflects a pleasure in its creation which the latter does not. Best of all, of course, would be the coupling of the real accuracy of the one with the imagined enthusiasm of the other. But there can be little question as to precedence: pleasure and enthusiasm must be the first (and at times the only) goal of the English teacher. Literature chosen for the English class should be selected by the prime criteria of immediate interest and particular relevance to the students' situation. The important question to be asked is, "What *will* they read?" and not, "What *should* they read?" If teachers of English view themselves first as purveyors of pleasure rather than as instructors in skill, they may find that skill will flourish where pleasure has been cultivated.

One implication of teaching literature from a social rather than a literary point of view is that the English class will combine language training and social studies. This view of teaching literature finds the English-Social Studies "core" curriculum one of the most reasonable of modern educational structures. It is based upon the realization that all effective literature is related to life in the same way that a portrait is related to its subject: If the living object is caught and interpreted at a vital moment, viewers will examine the portrait and read the literature because of their informing relationships to life. Such information is the pleasurable first engagement that leads toward later study and understanding. In the same way, reading materials selected for their actual and potential relevance to the student's own experience are likely to be twice valuable: once for the absorbing interest in self which they invite, an interest bound to promote a greater desire to read; and again for understanding and acceptance of the social norm, an attitude which it is any school's chief business to promote.

A further implication of a combined English-Social Studies class is reliance upon a daily newspaper as one of the chief texts of the course. The newspaper is in many ways an ideal text for the English class; its format, style, and content all qualify it as an excellent vehicle for teaching reading and writing with special attention to the social point of view. The sense of informality and immediacy which the very presence of the newspaper conveys, a sense so useful and so difficult to discover in many other kinds of literature, is also communicated in many magazines and soft-bound, pocket-sized books. Each of these three types of literature provides readily available materials designed to engage the most reluctant reader; each therefore commends itself for considerable and continuing use in the English class.

After a good deal of trial, and considerable error, the English teachers at both the Maxey and Garnet-Patterson Schools have derived formulas for the use of newspapers and magazines which appear to satisfy the needs of teacher and pupil at both institutions. With the customary hyperbole of the theoretician, to whom the problems of distribution and collection never existed, I asked myself why the newspaper could not be used every day in every English classroom. Finding no answer that seemed negative enough to discourage the idea, I stipulated such usage as part of the original Maxey plan. It worked. When that plan was adapted to the needs of the public school, the formula of daily usage for the newspaper remained unchanged. It didn't work, and the teachers soon told me why:

At the training school, no class has yet had more than twelve boys in it. Although one BTS boy may be a teaching burden equivalent to four public school children, he possesses only one pair of hands (however quick) and he sits at only one desk (however disarrayed). Getting a dozen newspapers out and back is not usually very much of a task even for the inefficient classroom manager. But when that number of hands and desks is multiplied by three and more, then the job of distribution becomes considerably more formidable. This is especially true when the newspaper proves greatly attractive to the less able student, who gives it up as slowly as possible because he seldom has time to read all he wants.

A considerable number of teachers in the junior high school found that managing the newspaper in their classroom was becoming increasingly difficult. One result was the increase of classroom newspaper time beyond reasonable proportions. Allowing the children to continue their reading was easier than battling them for the newspaper, especially when so many of them were reading enthusiastically (or even just reading) for the first time. The answer to the problem was a change in the basic formula for use of both newspapers and magazines. Instead of employing the newspaper on a daily basis, and the magazine twice weekly, the two types of periodicals are now alternated so that newspapers are used three days a week and magazines twice. In order to decrease distribution problems still further, in most classes the two are seldom used on the same day.

> (2) *That the English teacher be encouraged to select
> and to create his own reading materials within the
> limits of type and format prescribed by this program.*

One of the most common and most serious flaws in programs for poor readers is the relationship between the teacher and the text(s) he uses to engage his students in the reading process. If the instructor does not take pleasure in the texts he uses, what then is the likelihood of pleasurable response from the pupil? The answer is not only obvious in the abstract, but all too obvious as well in schools I have visited where texts were apparently chosen with neither the particular teacher nor the poor reader in mind. With these observations as a guide, I have refrained from prescribing classroom materials and have limited my specific suggestions to matters of type, format, and style; I do not believe that desirable results will be obtained unless English teachers are offered a freedom of selection of materials which allows them to consider both the students' needs and their own inclinations.

This recommendation also speaks of having the English teacher "create" his own reading materials. Stories, plays, and essays written by the teacher who knows what his students' vocabulary really is, rather than what it should be; who knows particular facts rather than patent generalizations about their background, environment, and aspirations; who knows, in short, his students as individuals rather than types—such reading materials could be of unequalled value in engaging any student in the process of reading and writing. In response to the objection that few people, even teachers of writing, are effective creative writers, the answer must be made that anyone who can tell a child a bedtime story or recount a narrative he has read in a newspaper, book, or magazine, can create stories, plays, and essays appropriate as teaching devices. Any teacher who has not written such materials before is likely to be very pleasantly surprised at the ease with which he can create them and the readiness with which they are accepted by his students. In cases where teachers feel unequal to the demands of such a task, they may find their initial feelings of inadequacy dispelled by undertaking a writing project in cooperation with another instructor.

> (3) That the teaching of language skills be accomplished through organic rather than mechanic or descriptive means.

This recommendation is meant to influence a great variety of common practices in the English classroom. These practices range from spelling lists to workbooks of all kinds to schemes for analyzing sentence structures. What is wrong with one is wrong will all: they represent language in a condition of being rather than of doing. In that sense they are mechanic rather than organic, and they are self-defeating. They are always inefficient to some significant degree, but their inefficiency increases as the academic orientation of their student users decreases. This conclusion becomes inevitable when one considers the necessarily "practical" bias of the mind either unaccustomed or unable to abstract and transfer information. For such a mind, a real pleasure may be found in working up lists of properly spelled words. But unlike the pleasure of recognition in reading, which is likely to promote further reading and understanding, the pleasure which a student takes in a well-executed word list is not necessarily a satisfaction which causes those same words to be spelled correctly in sentences or even employed familiarly in written discourse. The student who can spell words when they are in lists, but who can neither use them nor spell them correctly when they are in sentences, is a familiar phenomenon in all classrooms. If a list is used at all in any classroom, it should be a list of sentences, a list of words doing rather than merely being, a list whose "carry-over" is guaranteed if only in a single instance for each word. Such a list would be an example of the organic method of teaching language skills which this program advocates.

A consistent employment of this approach would cause the workbook to undergo serious scrutiny. To begin with, there is the question of whether most workbooks are in fact accumulative. Do succeeding lessons really depend upon and build upon those which precede them? Or are the skills which the workbooks teach as fragmented as the workbooks themselves? These are unproved accusations, however, and reflect more suspicion than hard evidence. What is not mere suspicion is the great generic flaw of the workbook: it too readily permits itself to be viewed by teacher and pupil alike as a world unto itself, a repository of exercises which develop skills useful in working upon workbooks. Little evidence can be found to support the argument that the workbook participates in any meaningful relationship with the world in which language performs tasks more demanding than its own arrangement. Generations of students have exercised upon them and come away

71

in the flabbiest sort of verbal condition. Therefore this program recommends that the English curriculum replace the workbook with exercises composed by the classroom teacher, exercises which are free of the book-grouping that suggests they have a life of their own and which are aimed at strengthening observed and particular weaknesses rather than the normative and anticipated problems to which workbooks customarily direct themselves.

Schemes for analyzing sentence structures are subject to many of the same criticisms which question the usefulness of the workbook. Most damaging perhaps is the simple question of their relevance: that is, what do they tend to generate? Do they create understanding, or do they in fact merely recreate themselves? Does exercise of the schematic intelligence produce verbal understanding? We have all had students who take great pleasure in their ability to diagram a sentence, just as others enjoy making lists of spelling words. But even as a list of words in sentences removes one more mechanical barrier between learning and meaning, so does a sentence analyzed in sentences add the organic dimension to a previously mechanical diagram. The making of a sentence diagram is evidence for little more than the student's ability to learn and the teacher's ability to teach the practice of diagramming sentences. The writing of even a one sentence analysis is an altogether more convincing piece of evidence for the student's understanding of sentence structure.

A further illustration of the difference between an organic and a mechanic philosophy of teaching in the English classroom is the interesting example of the class-written story or play. What makes these exercises especially remarkable in the usual curriculum is their total absence. Stories and plays are of course employed with great frequency; but as the creation of others, they are far more likely to inspire the reluctant reader and writer to an interest in content rather than in form. That this interest in content is desirable, especially in an English class which emphasizes social studies, is undeniable; but that it need be at the expense of an interest in form is not so clear. If the student has a "practical" rather than an abstractive mind, give him the first-hand experience he needs to learn from. Let the words be occasionally his own: let him witness words doing as he uses them to make a story or a play. Let him have the always-pleasing experience of creating an art form, whether artful or not. Any reservations on the instructor's part about the capacity of his class for such a performance are likely to disappear in the face of their enthusiasm. The group nature of the undertaking is usually efficient in quieting individual fears, so much so that students who would ordinarily never consider creative expression are sometimes brought to try a piece of writing themselves. And, most important, many members of the group discover what a sentence is by making one, and thus discovering what it does.

The conclusion both to this chapter and to the theory of this program is appropriately furnished by a specific example of the program in action. The following three week study guide for *West Side Story,* written by Miss Ann Farnell for her English and Social Studies classes at Maxey School, is included here as a model for use of paperbound books in the classroom. This particular study guide has the strongest possible recommendation—it works. It has been used by all English and Social Studies teachers at BTS, with invariably good results. The premises upon which the guide is based are those same premises upon which the program is founded: Begin with material students like, then relate that material to their life outside the confines of the classroom. If, as teachers, we can export general values by importing particular environments, we have a clear and present duty to create those environments within our classrooms. No argument for "quality" can be as persuasive as this conclusion quoted from the report on *Paperbound Books in New Jersey Public Schools:*

> *"It was found that the so-called reluctant reader and the slow learner were not so reluctant or as slow as certain teachers previously thought. Provided with books that interested them, they were no longer reluctant or slow. Over and over again, these stu-*

dents concluded that they learned more by reading something they liked. . . . It was found that the near-illiterates in many classrooms were now reading whole books albeit that many of these selections would not be considered meritorious from a literary point of view. Nevertheless, they were reading and enjoying this new experience."

West Side Story was chosen by Miss Farnell as the subject of the first of her study guides because she had seen it, read it, and liked it. She was, in short, applying the same criteria of familiarity that she hoped would engage her students. Where her familiarity was vicarious, theirs might be first-hand. But she was sure that whether read or lived, the experiences of the people in *West Side Story* were real enough to her students to engage their interest and universal enough to teach any young reader (and some older ones) valuable lessons about himself and his world.

Teachers will notice how careful Miss Farnell has been to relate the book to the lives of her students. In order to use her study unit as it was meant to be used—and as it has subsequently proven so successful—"Daily Objectives" must invariably be combined with "Enrichment Activities" which are keyed to the same page divisions as the "Objectives." Where daily objectives focus the student's attention on the book itself, they are less important than the enrichment activities which make every effort to give the book a vitality that can come only from the pulse of reality. If it's "just a story," it's likely to be just no good. Bring alive the situation and the characters who people it, and no book can be resisted by any student with even minimal abilities to perceive meaning.

The last page of the study guide deserves particular attention. This list of over twenty books represents Miss Farnell's attempt to give *West Side Story* wider experiential implications than one novel or one play can itself contain. To accomplish this, she has created a temporary classroom library of books dealing centrally and in every degree of tangent with the concerns of *West Side Story*. Her experience, and the experiences of others who have used this guide as a pattern, is that no device more effectively creates willing readers than one good book with others like it easily and immediately available.

THREE WEEK STUDY GUIDE FOR

WEST SIDE STORY

*Published by Pocket Books, Inc., 630 Fifth Ave., New York, New York 10020.

by Irving Shulman

Ann C. Farnell, English Teacher
W. J. Maxey Boys Training School
Whitmore Lake, Michigan

INTRODUCING THE BOOK

Since *West Side Story* has been widely shown as a movie, the sound track played frequently on the radio and as part of personal record collections, the music sung and danced on television, teachers will probably find that many of their students have some recognition of the title. This can be a handicap, for some students will respond negatively because they feel that they know the material. The teacher can capitalize on this, however, by encouraging those very students to tell a little about what they know. After brief discussion, the teacher can disclose something unique about this book that most students are unlikely to know: That the book is a novelization of the play which was adapted to a movie. The more usual arrangement is to have the book written first, and then to have a play or a movie made from it. But in this case, the teacher can point out, the play was so good that the public wanted and got a novel based upon it.

This is also a good opportunity to touch on *West Side Story* as an operetta where the important dialogue is sung and the scenes danced rather than spoken and acted. The teacher can remind the class that even though the situation centers around teenage gangs in the big city, and singing and dancing may seem inappropriate to a fight scene, this is just one other way of expressing a real life situation. The reality is simply enhanced by the pace and drama of the singing and dancing. Here, however, lies the big advantage of reading the book for those students who were repelled by the movie. The book of course is entirely without singing and dancing. It is a novel, it is written like a novel, and it reads like any other good story.

West Side Story

OVERALL OBJECTIVES:
1. To show how fear and dissatisfaction with oneself and one's way of living cause:
   A. Some people to try to change the status quo;
   B. Other people to fight tooth and nail to maintain it.
2. To show that fear and dissatisfaction cause:
   A. Some people to group together in order to protect their interests;
   B. Other people to come together to try to better their lives.
3. To show how fear and dissatisfaction cause:
   A. Some people to "go along" even though they don't really approve;
   B. Other people to try to break away.
4. To show how the same motivations of fear and dissatisfaction were the conditions that created the two gangs.
5. To show how failure to recognize and understand their similarities caused them only to see their differences.
6. To show how hatred is a result of dissatisfaction, fear, frustration, lack of love, failure to recognize similarities, and relentless concentration on differences.
7. To show how two individuals were temporarily able to overcome their personal fears and group frustrations to love each other.
8. To show how the gang's collective hatred caused them to destroy the individual love of Tony and Maria.
9. To show how common hatred led to a common tragedy.
10. To show how hate, instead of solving problems, only creates more hatred, more problems, and finally leads to tragedy.
11. To show the close relationship between ignorance and prejudice, and ignorance and fear.
12. To encourage investigation of one's own attitudes toward other people.

13. To encourage empathy or "putting yourself in the other person's shoes."

14. To show how the needs for acceptance, status, and recognition are traits basic to all human beings.

15. To show how friendship can be abused and used selfishly.

16. To show how vengeance only makes things worse in the long run.

17. To show how good intentions, if not thought-out carefully, can lead to tragedy for everyone.

18. To encourage personal comparison of one's own feelings with story book characters.

19. To show that literature, music, art, plays, and movies are expressions of situations that usually are true to life.

20. To encourage oral, written, graphic, and dramatic expression.

DAILY OBJECTIVES

1. To see the personal conflicts within the Jets.
   A. Action vs. Riff
   B. Riff vs. Tony
   C. Baby-Face vs. the gang
   D. Anybody's vs. the gang
2. To see the conditions that create gangs.
   A. Dissatisfaction
   B. Fear
   C. No Direction
3. To see the attitudes that permit gangs to flourish.
   A. The landlord and other tenants
   B. The police

DISCUSSION QUESTIONS

1. Who is Riff Lorton?
2. List as many members of the Jets as you can find in the first chapter.
3. How is Tony "different" from the Jets now?
4. How has Tony both disappointed and helped Riff?
5. If Action wants to be the leader of the Jets, why doesn't he challenge Riff?
6. What are both Baby-Face and Anybody's trying to do in reference to the gang?
7. How do the landlord and other tenants feel about the Jets vs. the Puerto Ricans?
8. Even though Sergeant Krupke and Detective Schrank question the Jets about the stink bomb, how do they really feel about Puerto Ricans?
9. How do Schrank and Krupke feel about their jobs and the kind of job they are doing?

Study Sheet II
Chapter One, pp. 17-22
West Side Story

DAILY OBJECTIVES

1. To see why people leave their native countries to come to a new country.
   A. Living conditions in Puerto Rico
   B. Living conditions in New York
   C. Hopes carried to the new country (Maria)
   D. Reality of the new country (Bernardo)
2. To see how the Puerto Ricans cling together, just as the Jets do, but for different reasons.
   A. Family unity
   B. Same nationality
   C. Lack of acceptance by the majority
   D. Protection within the minority

DISCUSSION QUESTIONS

1. List at least three reasons why the Puerto Ricans left their native country to come to New York City.
2. From Bernardo's and Maria's conversation on the roof, what ideas do you get about their family life?
3. How does Maria feel about being in America?
4. In contrast, how does her brother Bernardo now feel about being in America?
5. Do you think Bernardo probably had the same attitude as Maria when he first came? Why do you think so?
6. Since Puerto Rico is a territory of the United States and Puerto Ricans are considered American citizens, do you think Bernardo has a right to be so bitter? Explain your answer.
7. If you were Bernardo, do you think you would feel the same? Why?
8. What do you think the saying "Misery loves company" means? How does this saying apply to the Jets and Sharks?

9. What do you think the saying "Blood is thicker than water" means? Can this saying apply to the Jets and Sharks? How?

DAILY OBJECTIVES

1. To see how Tony was trying to break away from the Jets.
2. To see how Riff used friendship to pressure Tony.
3. To see how Doc and Senora Mantanios had similar problems.
   A. Doc and Tony
   B. Senora Mantanios and Maria
   C. Their stores
4. To see the basis of Anita's and Maria's friendship.
   A. Maria is Bernardo's sister
   B. Both are Puerto Ricans
5. To see Maria's dissatisfaction with Chino.

MATCHING QUESTIONS AND ANSWERS

Directions: In the underlined blanks write the letter of the answer that best completes the statement.

1. Tony decides to quit the Jets because_____.
2. Riff gets the Jet's leadership because_____.
3. "Blood is thicker than water" could apply to both _____ and_____.
4. Doc complains about iron shutters over the store windows because_____.
5. Tony attributes the shutters to_____.
6. Riff tells us he's in a gang because_____.
7. Senora Mantanios wants the doors locked and the shutters closed because_____.
8. All the characters in this section are similar because _____.
9. Maria is dissatisfied because_____.

— — — — —

A. otherwise you don't belong, you're nowhere, and belonging puts you on top of the world.
B. of Tony's and Riff's friendship.
C. of discontent at the sense of inferiority, of being ignorant, which cool talk couldn't change.
D. of Tony's and Doc's friendship.
E. of all gangs and their destructiveness.
F. Tony has passed it on.
G. of Maria's and Anita's friendship.
H. of the Anglos.
I. others' desires seem more important than her own.
J. the P.R.'s.
K. they are trying to protect their interests.

DAILY OBJECTIVES

1. To see the role of Murray Benowitz, the social worker.
    A. His hopes about the value of his work
    B. The realities he didn't expect
    C. His frustrated, but continued will to help
2. To see how Tony's values changed enough to allow him to be attracted to a Puerto Rican.
3. To see how Maria's prejudice toward Americans was too weak to ignore Tony.
4. To see how even passive Chino overcame his fear when his interest (Maria) was threatened.
5. To see how Bernardo protected his interest (Maria), but became enraged because she "crossed" the gang line.

DISCUSSION QUESTIONS

1. Why had Murray Benowitz's other neighborhood dances failed?
2. How had his experiences with these kids changed his view of the world?
3. If you were Murray Benowitz, would you have kept trying to better things? Explain your answer fully.
4. What emotion did Maria first experience when Tony danced with her?
5. Why was Maria afraid?
6. Up to now, what kind of picture do we have of Chino? How does this picture change when he sees Maria with Tony?
7. Do you think Bernardo should have gotten so angry with Maria? Explain your answer.
8. If you were Tony, would you have left Maria alone rather than get involved? Explain your answer.

DAILY OBJECTIVES

1. To see how Tony tries to solve the gangs' problems and his personal conflicts.
   A. Persuade the gangs to fight one-to-one or not at all
   B. Make Maria happy by arbitrating
2. To see how Riff's loyalty to Tony gave Bernardo the opening to vent his hatred.
3. To see how frustrated love, bravery, and friendship add fuel to fear and hatred.
4. To see the tragic results of tormented emotions.

DISCUSSION QUESTIONS

1. In the Coffee Pot, how did the Jets act? What was their spirit and feeling about the coming fight?
2. How did Tony suggest the fight should be handled? Why?
3. Why did Tony show up at the fight? What did he intend to do?
4. What events thwarted his good intentions?
5. He soon realized he might have handled things differently. What did he realize he could have done if he had thought more clearly?
6. What were the final results of the fight?

Study Sheet VI
Chapters Seven, Eight, Nine and Ten,
pp. 95-120
West Side Story

DAILY OBJECTIVES

1. To see the after-effects of the fight on everyone else.
    A. Maria and Tony
    B. Chino and Anita
    C. The other Jets
2. To see how futile revenge is as a problem solver.
3. To see how good intentions are not enough.
4. To see how the final tragedy was shared by all.

DISCUSSION QUESTIONS

1. What changes did Maria go through in her feelings about Tony after learning he killed her brother?
2. Why did Chino really kill Tony? To avenge Bernardo's death, to avenge his rejection by Maria, or both? Explain your answer.
3. If you had been Chino, what would you have done?
4. How did the other Jets feel about Tony afterward?
5. How did the other Jets feel about themselves and the whole incident later?
6. In Chapter Nine, when Maria and Tony are talking about Riff, what new discoveries do they make about Riff's and Tony's friendship? How do they decide Riff and Bernardo are alike?
7. What do they conclude about Riff's and Bernardo's futures if they had lived?
8. Why does Maria feel Tony was not doomed to the same destiny as Riff and Bernardo?
9. Why then is Tony's death the real tragedy in this tragic story?
10. How does Anita try to prove her strong friendship for Maria?
11. Anita's intentions, like Tony's, were good when she

left the drugstore. What happened to cause her to change her mind? What was the result? Why did she change the message? What could she have done instead?

12. What is the meaning of the last sentence on page 120, "And if things did not change, was this the way it would always be?"

ENRICHMENT ACTIVITIES

A. Chapter One, pp. 1-16

1. Write a character sketch of either Detective Schrank or Officer Krupke. What kind of men are they? What are their goals and ambitions? How do they feel about themselves, their work, the neighborhood, each other, the kids, the city, Puerto Ricans, etc.?
2. Draw a picture illustrating any incident in the first chapter which interests you.
3. Make a list with definitions of vocabulary words from the first chapter which you were not familiar with before. Keep the list up to date as you read. Hand in the list as a vocabulary booklet after you have finished the novel.
4. Describe a time when you felt or experienced thoughts or events like those of the characters in the first chapter.
5. Draw a group or individual picture (in words) of the various characters mentioned in the first chapter.

B. Chapter One, pp. 17-22

1. Write a report on the history of Puerto Rico.
2. Find out as much as you can about the words "prejudice," "scapegoat," and "status quo." Find out for yourself what they mean, then take a poll of the people around you and see how many other people know what they mean. Keep track of the right and wrong answers that you get. Also record the age of the people you poll.
3. Find out what a minority group is and write a report on the history of a minority group in this country.
4. Keep a scrapbook for a few weeks of any incidents you find in the newspaper of prejudice encountered or progress made by a minority group in obtaining their rights.

C. Chapters Two, Three and Four, pp. 22-69
  1. Keep a list of the Spanish words you find throughout the story and look up their meanings.
  2. Write a description of someone who reminds you of any of the characters in the story without giving his real name.
  3. Write a report on Social Work and what social workers do.
  4. Draw a map of Puerto Rico giving information as to its size, population, major products, industries and agriculture, government, and distance from New York City.
  5. Try to find information as to other locations in the United States with a heavy minority group population. For example, California and Washington have large Oriental populations. Give some statistics such as numbers of people, when most came to the U.S., and why.
D. Chapters Five and Six, pp. 70-95
  1. Give an oral or written report on a time when you were afraid. What events led up to the situation. How did you feel? What did you do about it? If you could, would you handle the situation in the same way? If not, how else would you handle it?
  2. Write a newspaper article reporting the deaths of Bernardo and Riff. Give a little history as to the cause of the gang fight and how these fights can be prevented in the future.
  3. Tell about a time you were involved in a similar incident. What led up to it and what were the results.
  4 Tell or write about why Riff's and Bernardo's deaths are considered tragic. How do you think this will affect the rest of the characters in the story?
E. These Concluding Activities cover the whole book:
  1. Form small groups and reenact any of the major scenes in the story. Act out what took place in the story, and then act out your own version of

how the situation could have been handled so
nobody got hurt.

2. Write an analysis of the various friendships de-
scribed in the story. What is friendship to you?
How far does a person go for a friend? How
were friendships abused in the story? Compare
Anita's and Maria's friendship with Tony's and
Riff's.

3. Give oral reports on parts of the story that especially interested you. For example, some of these
parts might be: prejudice, love, hate, revenge,
dissatisfaction, status, hope, acceptance, kind-
ness. If you choose one of these, you could tell
what these words mean to you and use various
characters from the story to support your ideas.

4. Write or tell about how you felt when you had
finished the story. Did it affect you personally in
any way? Did you feel sorry for anyone? If so,
why? What parts made you feel happy?

5. Not much attention is paid in the story to the
mothers of Doc and Tony. How do you think
they felt afterward? Support your views by including the information available about these
people.

6. Write another version of how the story could
have ended. How would you have liked to have
seen it end?

7. Give oral or written book reports on any books
you read that you think could be related to this
story. Tell what you think the relationship is between the book you read and this story.

8. Form a group and draw a mural depicting some
of the major scenes from the book.

9. Write or tell about a gang you know and some
of their activities.

10. Form a panel to discuss gangs.

11. Write your own version of *West Side Story*
using some real life people you are acquainted
with.

SAMPLE DAILY LESSON PLAN

West Side Story

FIRST WEEK

Lesson	*Homework*
Day One: Introduce book and review Overall Objectives with class. Begin reading Chapter 1.	Finish Chapter 1.
Day Two: Review Study Sheet I. Write out Study Sheet I. Explain Enrichment Activities. Group to select activities to be started tonight.	Start Enrichment. Continue reading.
Day Three: Discuss Study Sheet I. Introduce Study Sheet II. Review Objectives. Write out Study Sheet II.	Finish Study Sheet II. Continue reading; work on Enrichment Activities.
Day Four: Discuss Study Sheet II. Work on Enrichment Activities. Or, introduce Study Sheet III (if using S.S. III as test, Chapters 1-3 to be read by tomorrow).	Read Chapters 1-3. Work on Enrichment Activities.
Day Five: Review Study Sheet III—to be done in class or used as either open- or closed-book test. Pass out Study Sheet IV for homework.	Study Sheet IV and Enrichment Activities due Day Six.

SECOND WEEK

Day Six: Hand in Enrichment Activities. Discuss Study Sheet IV. Pass out Study Sheet V and review.

Read Chapters 5 and 6. Complete Study Sheet V.

Day Seven: Discuss Study Sheet V. Choose Enrichment Activities again. Work in class.

Work on Enrichment Activities. Read Chapters 7 and 8.

Day Eight: Continue Enrichment Activities. Pass out and review Study Sheet VI. Start Study Sheet VI.

Continue reading Chapters 9 and 10; work on Enrichment Activities due Day 10.

Day Nine: Continue Study Sheet VI discussion. Work on Enrichment Activities.

Work on Enrichment Activities.

Day Ten: Hand in Enrichment Activities. Finish discussion. Motivate for Concluding Activities.

THIRD WEEK

Day Eleven: Work on Concluding Activities. Begin presentations on Day Thirteen.

Day Twelve: Continue Concluding Activities.

Day Thirteen: Begin presentations.

Day Fourteen: Presentations.
Day Fifteen: Presentations.

RELATED READING

The books listed below relate directly or indirectly to *West Side Story* and can be found in the classroom library while we are studying that novel.

AUTHOR	TITLE
Elizabeth Kytle	WILLIE MAY
Louisa Shotwell	ROOSEVELT GRADY
Ethel Waters	HIS EYE IS ON THE SPAR-ROW
Richard Griffin	BLACK LIKE ME
Richard Wright	BLACK BOY
Richard Wright	NATIVE SON
Richard Wright	UNCLE TOM'S CHILDREN
Harry Golden	MR. KENNEDY AND THE NEGROES
Martin Luther King, Jr.	WHY WE CAN'T WAIT
Louis Lomax	WHEN THE WORD IS GIVEN
Louis Lomax	THE NEGRO REVOLT
Chester Himes	THE THIRD GENERA-TION
Harper Lee	TO KILL A MOCKING-BIRD
James Baldwin	GO TELL IT ON THE MOUNTAIN
James Baldwin	THE FIRE NEXT TIME
James Baldwin	BLUES FOR MISTER CHARLIE

James Baldwin	NOBODY KNOWS MY NAME
Martin L. Duberman	IN WHITE AMERICA
Ralph Ellison	THE INVISIBLE MAN
Michael Dorman	WE SHALL OVERCOME

MOTIVATION AND LEARNING

Morton H. Shaevitz, Ph.D.
Department of Psychology
University of Michigan

Interaction between student and teacher, one of the critical elements in the educational process, can be a mutually frustrating experience. The teacher who may initially be enthusiastic is often baffled by bored or indifferent responses and eventually becomes angry, resentful, or simply defeated. The student who senses this undertone in the classroom dialogue successfully resists all blandishments. Such a confrontation can only have unfortunate results: Students move through classes waiting for the escape that comes at the end of the day, the end of the year, or the end of the legal requirement for education. Teachers find themselves performing minimally and automatically; the sense of excitement they once had has disappeared.

This cycle of mutual despair can be broken only if we understand how it develops: Children come to school with a set of feelings that can range from excited anticipation through reluctant acquiescence to fearful and angry dread. The more negative the feelings, the more important that the child be reached quickly and effectively. If the frightened and angry child is to profit from his school years, his experience must differ sharply from his expectations. Too often, however, the one reinforces the other, and the child's fear and anger become a communicable classroom disease, infecting teacher and other pupils alike.

When educators talk about "motivating" a child, they often mean trying to change how he feels about an activity either by offering rewards for action or by placing the activity in a different context so that it seems more closely related to his current interests. Rewards that teacher bestow are customarily in the form of recognition or praise and depend upon the child's desire to be liked by the teacher. The teacher's effectiveness usually decreases with time, however, and often becomes insufficient by itself to counter the child's negative reaction to what he regards as a distasteful task. But if appeals can be made to the interests and needs that the child brings to the classroom, the teacher's approval can strengthen the intrinsic satisfaction which the child experiences in performing any pleasurable activity.

The individual who enjoys reading, reads constantly. Books, newspapers, magazines—whenever he has a free moment, his reading begins. One apparently reasonable assumption is that the man who reads so avidly must be highly conscious of the pleasure that reading gives him. Rather surprisingly, perhaps, this is generally not true. For the individual who finds pleasure in it, the act of reading seems to satisfy so many needs that it becomes almost reflexive. When presented with something to read, his automatic response is to reach for it. This response is basically what is meant by having a positive attitude toward books and reading.

The goal of a literacy training program must be the development of positive attitudes toward reading and writing. This can best be accomplished by having the child discover that his needs can be satisfied by these activities. School should provide him not only with experience of new things, but also with opportunity to find out more about those things that are important to him. If this is accomplished within the context of an educational activity, the activity itself begins to be meaningful and rewarding. This in turn leads to the increased probability that the child will pursue the activity for his own satisfaction.

Reading Mechanics

The past thirty years have been characterized by controversy about the most efficient and least painful ways to teach the basic mechanics of reading. Teachers are familiar with whole word, phonics, kinesthetic, look and see, and all combination methods, each of which has been vigorously championed. An over-view of the field gives a startling conclusion: No matter what method is used, most children will learn the mechanics of reading fairly well. Conversely, no matter what method is used, a small but persistent percentage of children will not be able to learn by any single method of instruction. For these students a method different from that which the child has found unsuccessful must be employed. It is at the point where the child is *able* to read that the nature of his experience is likely to determine whether or not he *will* read.

Little or no problem may be encountered in dealing with the child who comes from a home environment where reading is highly valued and where adults pursuing books for pleasure and for profit are a familiar sight. The probability is high that the reading he does in the classroom is merely a small part of his total environment of written material and that he has only been waiting to be taught to read before he will pursue books on his own. Usually, he wants to achieve, he is rewarded for reading, and he will read avidly and widely with or without the school's help. Recent experience with gifted classes has shown that the best way to deal with these students is to give them what they ask for, give them some direction, and then get out of the way.

The student I am concerned with, however, can be described as having any or all of the following characteristics: (1) intellectual level below average to slightly above average (80-105); (2) a home environment where books are not in evidence and where parents seldom read; (3) school achievement in the early grades inadequate or marginal. These students, who comprise at least 50% of the public school population, may be those destined to become non-literate. These are the students who often grow up seeing books as enemies to be avoided and obstacles to be surmounted, but rarely if ever as objects that can be gratifying, fulfilling, and exciting in themselves.

Standard educational practices are most often damaging to students who have intellectual or motivational barriers to overcome. Such students must be exposed to situations that are maximally stimulating early in their educational history or they will have no future place in a learning environment. If the child is forced to deal with materials that are either uninteresting or irrelevant to his current existence, then the chances are greatly increased that he will learn to regard the activity with anger or anguish.

When special books for teaching children *how* to read were first developed, great emphasis was placed on keeping the material simple and highly repetitive. The principle of providing an opportunity for continual review is appropriate if the child is motivated to learn. But for the child who is ambivalent about school, the utilization of these scientifically sound but unbearably dull materials convinces him that reading is another activity to be endured.

Educators have recognized recently that the child's needs for novelty, stimulation, and a context for identification should be met by the content of the earliest written material with which he is taught. Education has made a slow but persistent movement toward the use of primary material that is adventurous, includes relevant illustrations, and develops themes that are contemporary and interesting. This trend must continue.

Reading Strategy

Teachers have always been struck by the differences in the thirty or more children who enter their classrooms each day. Yet somehow this uniqueness is forgotten when the reading period begins. The variety of reasons for which a child may perform is often overlooked. Perhaps he admires the teacher and wants his approval, or he is frightened of the teacher and of the consequences of failure. Perhaps the activity itself has pleasurable aspects for him. Of these three alternate possibilities, only the third can be the goal of a viable reading program. If one expects the child to read

101

not because he wishes to please, not because he is frightened of displeasing, but specifically because he finds reading a pleasurable, satisfying, and sustaining activity, then the child's experience with written material must be so rewarding that only positive attitudes can be the result.

The greater variety of reading material available, the greater likelihood that some of it will appeal to the child's interests. The greater variety, the greater likelihood that the child's constantly shifting attention can be captured, and the greater likelihood that books, magazines, and newspapers will become more and more a part of the child's natural existence. The first prerequisite of a literacy program is to give the child enough material so that he can find the things that he likes and like the things that he finds.

In the early 1900's nutritionists, pediatricians, and psychologists were concerned with the development of proper eating habits in children. Rigid scheduling of meal-times was stressed, as was the necessity for making sure that every meal was well balanced and provided the basic nutritional essentials. The child was bombarded with demands that he eat when food was presented. Only upon re-examination was the folly of this approach recognized. What was momentarily forgotten was that children get hungry, and when hungry will actively seek out food. By introducing constraints and emphasizing the task elements of the activity, the pleasurable aspects of eating were overshadowed. The justification for continued harassment was the assumption that it was being done in the interests of the child.

Except for cases of physical illness or severe psychological disturbance, no child has been known to voluntarily starve himself to death. Once the naturally pleasurable aspects of eating were ignored by parents, however, great problems were created. But it was not the children who were having an eating problem; it was the parents. Nonetheless, of course it was the children who suffered. One of the discoveries that caused the whole foolish practice of meal-time harassment to abate was that infants as young as one year would eat nutritionally balanced meals if they

102

were given a wide variety of foods and allowed to choose anything they wanted.

The analogy to reading is painfully obvious: The *pleasurable* aspects of reading must be experienced if a child is to develop attitudes toward reading that enable him both to survive and to profit from the learning experience. This means that he must begin to realize that reading can satisfy his psychological needs. Furthermore, the implication is clear that the limited choices offered children by present school reading materials *must* be increased so that the habit of reading will not die from eventual starvation.

But is it not the function of an educational system to introduce the child, adolescent, and young adult, to the best literature that is available? Is the system not charged with the obligation to make certain that what the student reads is good for him and has the secondary value of instilling in him a subjective appreciation of fine writing? The answer to this must be *NO!* if quality is taught at the price of assuring that the student will always regard reading as an activity which is performed at someone else's direction, and that this same student will habitually separate the activity of reading from the world in which he finds pleasure and enjoyment. If this child reads for his teacher, because of his teacher, and with his teacher, then the reading will disappear when the teacher does. When the teacher functions to provide stimulation rather than restriction, then both teacher and child will benefit.

Once mastery of mechanics and development of favorable attitudes have been accepted as equal goals in the teaching of literacy, the resourcefulness and creative potential of the teacher will find many new approaches. For example, often the most practical way of dealing with class size in the lower grades is to divide a class into small sections and work with these intensively. This assures that more attention will be given to each individual, and that each group will be of a manageable size. The most usual practice is to make this division on the basis of ability, with each group reading the same book at a different rate or each group reading about the same subject in books geared to subjectively different levels. Perhaps an alternate solution would be to group students according to *areas of interest,* a grouping which would increase their probable attendance to the reading lesson and therefore increase their probable rate and depth of comprehension.

In summary: An important goal of education is to assure that children develop a positive attitude toward reading. This can best be accomplished by: (1) modifying the attitudes of educators so that they become increasingly aware of motivational constructs and their importance in the process of learning and (2) discarding the beliefs that a child's education is dependent upon his exposure to distinguished literature and that the goal of a reading program is to assure that he has read such literature. This will lead to (3) an increased acceptance of a variety of reading materials as appropriate and even necessary to an adequate literacy program and (4) a constant searching for new and creative ways to make reading a pleasurable and meaningful activity for the student.

Writing

While reading is a solitary activity, writing should be viewed as interactional in nature. That is, it is a form of communication and is directed toward an object. In the case of the novelist, this object may be the world. In the case of the diarist, the object may be the person himself.

A student eventually may achieve pleasure from the mere fact of his own writing; initially, however, he must be shown how writing can be useful in his present environment. When the student is involved in a reading program that he enjoys, he will be more receptive to the idea that he can produce as well as ingest written material. Again, it is necessary to take advantage of his current interests and make assignments that are meaningful. He should be encouraged to write frequently since, as his skill increases, he will experience a concomitant rise in pleasure.

Another and perhaps even more important step is to increase the variety of circumstances in which the student is asked to write. Writing is too often an esoteric activity separated from the rest of the school program and performed routinely as an exercise. But any thoughtful teacher should be able to create situations where the student must write in order to satisfy his needs. The primary school teacher might say, "Please tell me in writing how you want to use the recess and I will choose the game from your suggestions." This illustrates the important condition of the teacher relating the child's written communication to his current existence.

Students at junior and senior high school levels traditionally write only in their English and Social Studies classes. This tradition has little to recommend it and should be violated for the sake of both student and curriculum. It should be possible to develop programs where students in Shop or Home Economics classes spend a small part of their time describing the next project they want to do and their reasons for doing it. Once the student realizes that he can get what he wants through the medium of writing, he is more likely to want to learn how to write.

I have addressed myself exclusively and deliberately to the question of pragmatic communication because the life circumstances and genetic and psychological factors that contribute to a person's ability to be a creative writer have not been isolated. Yet one thing is certain: creativity is not enough. The writer must have at his call vocabulary, context, and some idea of structure. Without them the tools of communication are lacking, and he lives in a world of frustration rather than production.

A final note on motivation directed to all those who correct a student's written work: Too much effort is expended upon indicating to the student what is wrong with his work and much too little in showing him what is right. What could be more discouraging than to get back a piece of paper covered with clear evidence of your incompetence? Far more useful to the teaching process would be a correctional procedure which emphasized whatever was competent in the paper more strongly than it emphasized the mistakes. One example might be to circle in bright red those sentences which are well constructed, in order to show the student that his teacher appreciates and can respond to those things that he does right as well as those that he does wrong. Parenthetically, it is much more efficient as a teaching device to indicate by example not only that something has been done wrong but also the right way to do it. That is, if the tense is wrong, insert the right form; if the sentence structure is incorrect, give an example of correct sentence structure; if the wording is awkward, show him a better way. This combination of indicating to the student the strengths of his performance as well as showing him how to correct his weaknesses will greatly increase the efficiency of the learning procedure. Not quite incidentally, the student may even look forward to having a paper returned.

Conclusion

If the goals of literacy training are to produce students who are able to read and enjoy reading, and who are able to write and enjoy writing, then some of the basic beliefs that educators hold, some of the techniques they use, and their awareness of motivational factors must change. If young adults are expected to be able to read in circumstances other than those of coercion, they must during their educational years experience reading as a pleasurable activity.

Effective writing is partially dependent upon sufficient practice. The student must see the relevance of written communication to his current attempts at environmental mastery. This mastery becomes an internalized need when he learns that he must be able to express himself clearly in order to get what he wants. Successful attainment of these desires would fulfill the needs and aspirations of educators and educated alike.

A NEW APPROACH TO EVALUATION

Morton H. Shaevitz, Ph.D.
Department of Psychology
University of Michigan

Creative approaches to education have greatly increased
in the past twenty years. These same years have been
marked by substantial increases in the minimal amount of
education necessary to compete successfully. Recognition
that education is critical for future achievement, that growing numbers of individuals must learn more than ever before, has encouraged the innovative efforts of educators,
social scientists, and scholars in related disciplines. Many
of these innovators have realized that one of the essential
elements in any educational endeavor is *literacy,* the functional ability to read and write. This realization has led
to great interest in the field of literacy training, but also to
a proliferation of untested and poorly substantiated claims.
Since the area is so crucial, great care must be taken to
determine if these claims have merit.

A traditional approach to evaluation has characterized
much of the earlier educational research. A new method
is introduced to students in one classroom while the standard method is used in another class. At the end of a specified period of time, performance tests are given to both
groups of students and the results compared. If the
performance of students being taught by the new method
is superior (and it usually is—novelty often leads to increased participation), the new method is adopted. Sub-
sequent testing often reveals regression to earlier performance until another "new" method is introduced, and the
cycle is repeated.

In the present research format, the traditional approach
has been rejected. First, English In Every Classroom is
directed toward the modification of *attitudes* toward read-

ing and writing with changes in performance expected to follow. This unique approach to literacy training demanded the development of new techniques that could be used to assess change. Second, because we were unwilling to assume that *any* educational program was best for *all* students, measures of individual difference were a clear necessity.

As English In Every Classroom developed, there was a concomitant emphasis on planning an evaluative approach to answer the myriad of questions that must be asked of this new and radical approach to education: (1) How are students affected by the program? (2) What types of students are most likely to be affected? (3) What types of changes can be expected? (4) Will there be a relationship between the modification of attitudes toward reading and writing and the development of greater skill? (5) How long lasting will the changes be?

The current program could not be easily introduced into a single classroom or even a selected number of classrooms in a school. Since the approach encompasses all aspects of the school situation and demands the cooperation of all faculty, an entire school was selected to serve as the experimental sample. In order to make certain that changes are a function of the unique experience that pupils are having within the new program, another school, similar in essential characteristics but continuing to function in its own way, was selected as a comparative group. Fortunately, Michigan has two boys training schools with similar characteristics. In only one of these schools was English In Every Classroom introduced.

The assessment of changes in attitudes toward reading and writing presents problems that are both practical and methodological. Attitudes are psychological constructs; that is, they cannot be directly observed but must be inferred from other behavior. Theoretically, an attitude can be defined as a relatively stable, predisposed way of responding to a set of related objects. If one were able to observe students attending both schools during all their waking hours and record how they responded to books, magazines, newspapers, or other printed material, the assessment of attitudes would be a simple matter. Since this procedure is impossible, one must obtain a sample of behavior which shows how students FEEL about reading and writing and infer attitudes as the psychological mechanisms which underlie these feelings.

Attitude Measures

Three test instruments are being used to measure attitudes toward reading and writing. The tests differ in the degree to which students report overt behavior. For example, in a *Behavior Rating Form* they are asked to identify whether or not they believe that each of 51 statements is self-descriptive by marking after each one LIKE ME or NOT LIKE ME. Most are general items such as (1) I'm pretty sure of myself; (2) I'm popular with kids my own age; (3) I can usually take care of myself. Amongst these questions are seven items that impinge directly on reading and writing:

1. Books are things I like to have around
2. I read a newspaper almost every day
3. I like to write things down then I think about them
4. I usually read something when I have some free time
5. I hate books
6. There are lots of magazines I am interested in
7. Writing is something I can do without

Initially, students in both schools are most likely to respond to these statements in ways which indicate negative attitudes. If the program of English In Every Classroom is successful, students participating in it should alter their responses as positive attitudes develop.

A second test which measures attitude change is called HOW MUCH DO YOU LIKE. Students are told that people differ in their liking for activities and in the degree to which they like them. They are then given a series of eight activities, followed by a bi-polar rating scale ranging from "like a little" to "like a lot." Amongst these items are four that relate directly to reading and writing:

1. Being in a school that has a library
   Like a little 1 2 3 4 5 6 7 Like a lot
2. Learning how to read and write well

109

Like a little 1 2 3 4 5 6 7 Like a lot
3. Reading books and magazines
   Like a little 1 2 3 4 5 6 7 Like a lot
4. Writing about things
   Like a little 1 2 3 4 5 6 7 Like a lot

In both of these tests the questions asked refer directly to reading and writing. What is expected is that for the students who read and write in a context that is interesting, stimulating, and satisfying (perhaps those students involved in English In Every Classroom), there will be a modification in attitude and increased reading and writing. This evaluation program is, of course, designed to show whether or not these changes do take place, and in what students they are most prominent. We hope also to show *how* attitudes change.

Reading is a word which denotes a specific type of activity, but it also has *connotative* meanings. Two students might offer identical definitions (denotative meaning), yet reading for one could be an activity that is interesting and important, while for the other it might be dull and unimportant. If a student changes his attitudes toward activities like reading and writing, this change should be reflected in modifications of the connotative meanings that these words have for him. For example, students at the Boys Training School in Michigan who are experimenting with English In Every Classroom have begun trading cigarettes for books. Since a cigarette is one of the few money-equivalents that the boys possess, and since they have themselves invented a system of "buying" desirable books from each other, one aspect of the connotative meaning of books that has changed has been *value*. If one were to ask these boys to rate the word BOOKS on a scale that ranged from Valuable to Worthless, books are likely to be valued more highly as the length of the boys' exposure to the program is increased.

This concept led to development of the Literacy Attitude Scale, a test which asks students to tell what they think about different words by rating them along specific dimensions. Previous work in the area of connotative

110

meaning[1] had shown that most words could be described by using three dimensions. These dimensions exist on a continuum from good to bad, powerful to weak, and active to passive. For example, most people would tend to rate the word BABY as being relatively good, active, and weak. The word WAR, by contrast, would be seen as bad, active, and strong. The questions to be answered by the Literacy Attitude Scale were whether words related to literacy training would change in meaning and along what dimensions they would change when students had been exposed to the experimental programs.

The scales being used to measure connotative meaning were chosen with multiple criteria in mind. Not only must they adequately sample the changes in meaning that concepts can undergo, but they must also make good sense to the student. In addition, the number of scales must be severely limited if the interest and participation of the students is to be ensured. Application of these criteria led to development of five scales intended to assess the student's attitude toward reading and writing. These five scales —good/bad, weak/strong, interesting/dull, small/big, important/unimportant—were then applied to twenty concepts (words to be rated). Of the twenty concepts, nine could be expected to reflect changes in attitude toward literacy. These key concepts are CLASSES, NEWSPAPERS, WRITING, READING, TESTS, TEACHERS, MAGAZINES, WORK, and BOOKS. Students also rate eleven other words such as FOOD, SPORTS, and CARS that would not be expected to change as a result of this program. The specific task is shown in the following example:

We would like to find out what you think about different things. At the top of each page is one word in capital letters. Use the spaces on the rest of the page to tell us what you think about that word. Here is an example:

At the top of the page you might see a word like

[1] Osgood, E. C., Suci, G. J., and Tannenbaum, P. *The Measurement of Meaning*. Urbana, Illinois: University of Illinois Press, 1957.

BOOKS

Then you will be asked to tell what you think about BOOKS. There are no right or wrong answers because everybody thinks different about different things. Maybe you think BOOKS are very bad. If you do, this is the way you would place your X.

1.___very good,___good,___sort of good,___not good or bad,___sort of bad,___bad, X very bad.

Now make up your own mind about using your X in the other four scales. Use only one X for each scale, don't leave out any scales, and place your X right on the line like this X.

BOOKS
ARE

2.___very weak,___weak,___sort of weak,___not weak or strong,___sort of strong,___strong,___very strong.
3.___Very interesting,___sort of interesting,___not interesting or dull,___sort of dull,___dull,___very dull.
4.___very small,___small,___sort of small,___not small or big,___sort of big,___big,___very big.
5.___very important,___important,___sort of important,___not important or unimportant,___sort of unimportant,___unimportant,___very unimportant.

The measurement of attitudes includes three separate yet related sets of questions. The first and, in a sense, most direct, asks that the student identify himself as someone who participates in activities related to reading and writing. The second asks how much he likes these activities. The third asks that he rate words related to literacy along *connotative* meaning dimensions. All measurements will be taken of students at both institutions. The first comparison that will be made is the difference in attitude change between students participating in English In Every Classroom and students being trained in a more usual manner. In addition to efforts to evaluate attitudinal changes in general, specific attempts will be made to identify the type of student most responsive to this program. The following section deals with the instruments used in this identification.

Student Characteristics

The three sources of information being used to describe student characteristics are diagnosticians' ratings, teachers' ratings, and students' self report. Each boy is tested individually by a clinical psychologist as part of the preparation for his stay at boys training school. (Most public schools also use the service of psychologists, but usually not for all students.) As a result of this testing, a general report of intellectual and emotional functioning is routinely prepared. It is often difficult, however, to extract relevant variables when large numbers of students are involved. Therefore, after psychologists have finished their reports, they are asked to complete a *Diagnostician's Evaluation Form*, which asks questions about the boys in three general areas: (1) degree and quality of emotional disturbance, (2) ability to form relationships and feelings of worth, and (3) initial attitude and probable behavior in classroom settings. Examples of the specific items follow:

1. Emotional Disturbance
   a. Evidence of a psychotic process
   none found __ __ __ __ __ __ __
                       probability for psychosis found
   b. Evidence of organic impairment
   Diagnosed significant
   impairment __ __ __ __ __ __ __ none
                                                      found

2. Relationships and Self Worth
   a. Pupils' capacity to form interpersonal relationships with peers
   high _ _ _ _ _ _ _ _ low
   b. Frustration tolerance
   becomes easily upset when
   frustrated _ _ _ _ _ _ _ _ rarely becomes upset
3. Attitudes and classroom behavior
   a. Probable relationship to teachers
   wanting to be accepted
   and liked _ _ _ _ _ _ _ resisting all overtures and maintaining a highly independent stance
   b. Probable attitude towards classroom limits
   accepts _ _ _ _ _ _ _ rebels

Teacher Observations

Teacher observations are customarily gathered in the form of a summary statement that varies with the individual teacher. Hence, comparison of students who have had different teachers is often difficult if not impossible. For this project, teachers are asked to rate their students on a number of characteristics both at the beginning and end of the academic year. A *Teacher's Evaluation Form,* similar in format to that used by the clinical psychologist but excluding items related to emotional functioning, is completed for each student. Teachers also complete a *Behavior Rating Sheet,* which is designed to make maximum use of the teacher's continuing and close interaction with the student. Fourteen bi-polar scales ask the teacher to make observations and inferences about the child that can be obtained from the classroom interaction. Examples follow:

Agile _ _ _ _ _ _ _ Awkward
Boisterous _ _ _ _ _ _ _ Shy
Withdrawn _ _ _ _ _ _ _ Outgoing

Low Intelligence __ __ __ __ __ __ __ High
                                        Intelligence
Energetic __ __ __ __ __ __ __ Lazy

Since the teachers evaluate their students early in the semester and again after having spent an extended period of time with them, changes in evaluation can then be related to changes in attitude and other related measures.

The final request for information from teachers is in the area of academic achievement. For ambivalent students, achievement tests often reflect more the level of participation than the level of ability. Teachers routinely see students perform at levels that are dissonant with their test scores. Here it will be important to observe whether teacher ratings are related to changes in attitude and also to discover what level of ability describes the student most responsive to English In Every Classroom.

Student's Self Report

The student's self report consists of a number of questionnaires that he completes at the beginning and end of the academic year. Two of these, the *Behavior Rating Form* and *How Much Do You Like,* were described previously when attitude measurement was discussed. A third test, related directly to the student's view of the classroom, attempts to measure his response to various scholastic situations ranging from tests to promotion. These three types of questionnaires combine to give an overall picture of how a student views himself, his likes and dislikes, and his expectations about school.

The second phase in the evaluation procedure is to compare these measures of student characteristics to determine if clusters of response emerge. Perhaps the largest shift in literary attitudes will occur in those students who are most anxious about school, who are believed by diagnosticians and teachers to have poor interpersonal relations, and who view themselves in very negative terms. Such identification would be the most important basis for selecting students to participate in a supportive program like English In Every Classroom.

Even though performance is not being stressed in the present program, modifications in attitudes toward reading and writing should inevitably lead to increased participation and, as practice continues, to greater skill. Often students are *able* to read interesting materials with apparent ease and are seemingly incapable of dealing with materials that fail to stimulate them. Reading tests may not reflect a student's ability, but merely his willingness to perform an assigned task. Nevertheless, measures of reading speed and comprehension are included in the evaluation program. The Stanford Achievement Test[2] is being administered to all students both at the beginning and end of the school year. It should tell us whether changes in attitudes toward reading as measured by questionnaires and increases in reading behavior as observed by teachers will be consonant with scores achieved on standardized tests. Previous experience in testing students who are uninterested in the standard reward that school bestows leads to the expectation that test performance will remain at a fairly low level and will *not* reflect actual changes in potential ability. New and different measures may have to be used if educators are to obtain an accurate estimate of potential.

While testing of reading ability is limited by students' participation in evaluative efforts, measurement of the ability to communicate in writing is even more complex. As students become more comfortable with words, they should develop a greater facility in using them. This hypothesis led to the desire to measure any change in the availability of verbal symbols to students participating in the program; therefore, a special instrument called the Verbal Proficiency Test was developed. Students are now being asked to list whatever uses they know or can imagine for a common item such as a milk carton, to make up as many words as possible using a fixed set of letters, to describe the consequences of an unexpected event such as the sudden ability of men to read each other's minds, to describe themselves along physical and emotional dimen-

2. *Stanford Achievement Test*, New York: World Book Co.

sions, and finally, to suggest improvements in items such as a bicycle or a chair. If the theory of increased facility is a viable one, then their performance on such tests before and after exposure to the program should be significantly different.

Conclusion:

This chapter has described an evaluation procedure devised specifically for the program of English In Every Classroom which has been instituted at the W.J. Maxey Boys Training School in Whitmore Lake, Michigan. These same procedures, appropriately modified, will be rigorously applied to the expansion of the program into the Model School Division of the District of Columbia Public Schools. This entire evaluative effort is based upon a philosophy of fusing program development and research which is meant to offer reasonably complete and thoroughly supportive answers to many of the difficult questions faced by teachers and curriculum planners in the teaching of literacy in the public school.

Summary Description of Test Instruments

I. Tests Students Take
   A. Stanford Achievement Test
      A well-known test of academic achievement. Measures of reading speed and reading comprehension are obtained.
   B. Verbal Proficiency Test
      A new instrument devised specifically for this project. Students are asked to list different uses for common items; to predict what would happen if specific environmental events occurred; to describe themselves; to make up as many words as possible using a fixed set of letters; and to suggest improvements in manufactured things.
   C. Literary Attitude Scale
      A new instrument devised specifically for this project. A modification of the semantic differen-

tial technique, it consists of 16 concepts on 5 bipolar scales. It measures the student's attitude towards various objects and activities by the connotative meaning that these things have for him.

D. How Much Do You Like?

A questionnaire asking the student to indicate his preference for various types of activities. Four of the items are particularly related to reading and writing behavior, and therefore will be used as a measure of attitude and attitude change.

E. Behavior Rating Form

A personality inventory which asks the student to react to a number of behavioral descriptions. Eight special items have been added to reflect responses toward books, other printed material, and general reading and writing behavior. This instrument will be used as another measure of possible attitude change and for various measures of self concept.

F. How Are Things in Class?

A questionnaire which asks the student to describe his response to various school situations.

II. Forms Teachers Complete

A. Teacher's Evaluation Form

A questionnaire developed for this project and designed to measure teachers' perceptions of students along both interpersonal and adjustment dimensions. A general descriptive sentence is followed by a bi-polar dimension and the teacher places the student along this dimension.

B. Teacher's Behavior Rating Sheets

A form that consists of 14 bi-polar dimensions anchored by antonymous adjectives. The task is to indicate the student's placement on each dimension.

C. Teacher's Achievement Rating

A form which asks the teacher to indicate a student's present achievement level in specific areas and his potential achievement in these same areas.

III. Form Diagnosticians Complete
  A. Diagnostician's Evaluation Form
     A nineteen item questionnaire similar in form to the Teacher's Evaluation Form but having diagnostic categories included.

IV. Demographic Data
  The following information will be recorded for each student: name, age, number of years school attended, most recent grade placement.

V. Post-Testing
  Six months after each boy in the testing sample is released from school he will be tested through his mandatory contact with his parole officer. Certain of the tests in the present battery are being modified and others are being devised to evaluate both attitude and performance in this post-institutional setting.

Summary of Testing Procedure

I. Test Students Take	Beginning	End
1. Stanford Achievement Test	X	X
2. Verbal Proficiency Test	X	X
3. Literary Attitude Scale	X	X
4. How Much Do You Like	X	X
5. Behavior Rating Form	X	X
6. How Are Things in Class	X	X
II. Teachers Fill Out		
1. Behavior Rating Sheet	X	X
2. Teacher's Evaluation Form	X	X
3. Teacher's Achievement Rating	X	X
III. Diagnosticians Fill Out		
1. Diagnostician's Evaluation Form	X	

FIVE HUNDRED PAPERBACK BOOKS
SELECTED BY TEENAGE READERS

assembled by
Daniel Fader, Ph.D.
Department of English
The University of Michigan

Author	*Title*	*Pub.*	*Price*
Adamson	Living Free	Macf.	.75
————	Born Free	Macf.	.75
Anderson	Pro Football Handbook	JLP	.50
Andrews	Quest of the Snow Leopard	Tempo	.50
Annixter	Buffalo Chief	Dell	.35
Armer	Screwball	Tempo	.50
Asimov	Caves of Steel	Pyr.	.40
————	I, Robot	Sig.	.50
Auerback	Basketball	PB	.35
Baldwin	Notes of a Native Son	Ban.	.60
————	The Fire Next Time	Dell	.50
————	Go Tell It on the Mountain	Dell	.60
————	Nobody Knows My Name	Dell	.50
————	Blues for Mr. Charlie	Dell	.60
Barlow	Black Treasure	Tempo	.50
Barrett	Lilies of the Field	Pop.	.40
Beach, S.	This Week's Stories of Mystery and Suspense	Berk.	.50
Beach, E. L.	Run Silent, Run Deep	PB	.50
————	Submarine	Sig.	.60
Benedict	Tales of Terror and Suspense	Dell	.45
Bennett	Great Tales of Action and Adventure	Dell	.40
Berg	Prison Nurse	Ban.	.40
Berra	Behind the Plate	JLP	.50
Berrill	The Living Tide	Prem.	.60
Bishop	The Day Lincoln Was Shot	PL	.85
————	A Day in the Life of President Kennedy	Ban.	.50
Bonham	War Beneath the Sea	Berk.	.45
————	Burma Rifles	Berk.	.50
Bowen	Hot Rod Angels	Nova	.45
Bradbury	Illustrated Man	Ban.	.50
————	Martian Chronicles	Ban.	.50
Brand	Folksongs for Fun	Berk.	.75
Brickhill	The Great Escape	Crest	.50
Buck	The Good Earth	PB	.50
————	Fighting Angel	PB	.50
Budrys	Rogue Moon	GM	.45
Bullock	Hitler, A Study in Tyranny	Ban.	.95
Bunn	Gus Wilson's Model Garage	Berk.	.45
Burgess	The Inn of the Sixth Happiness	Ban.	.50
Burnford	The Incredible Journey	Ban.	.50
Burroughs	Lost on Venus	Ace	.40
————	Beyond the Farthest Star	Ace	.40

Author	Title	Pub.	Price
————	Monster Men	Ace	.40
————	Mastermind of Mars	Bal.	.50
————	The Beasts of Tarzan	Bal.	.50
Campbell, J. W.	Astounding Tales of Space and Time	Berk.	.50
Campbell, R. W.	Drag Doll	Nova	.40
Canaway	A Boy Ten Feet Tall	Bal.	.50
Carell	Invasion: They're Coming	Ban.	.75
Carson	Silent Spring	Crest	.75
————	The Sea Around Us	Sig.	.60
Catton	Stillness at Appomattox	PB	.75
Cerf	Stories Selected from the Unexpected	Ban.	.50
Charnwood	Abraham Lincoln	PB	.35
Clark	To Goof or Not to Goof	Crest	.40
————	Your Happiest Years	PB	.50
Clarke	Earthlight	Bal.	.50
Coggins	Etiquette and Manners	Pyr.	.50
Colby	Weirdest People in the World	Pop.	.50
Collins	Moonstone	Pyr.	.60
Comics	Tales of the Incredible	Bal.	.50
Congdon	Combat: War with Germany	Dell	.60
————	Combat: War with Japan	Dell	.60
————	Combat: Pacific Theater—World War II	Dell	.60
————	Combat: European Theater—World War II	Dell	.60
Conklin	Invaders of Earth	Tempo	.50
————	Great Stories of Space Travel	Tempo	.50
————	12 Great Classics of Science Fiction	GM	.50
Connell	The Most Dangerous Game	Berk.	.45
Cooke	Man on a Raft	Berk.	.50
Coolidge	Hercules and Other Stories	SBS	.35
Coombs	Mystery of Satellite Seven	Tempo	.50
Cooper, J. F.	The Pathfinder	PB	.60
Cooper, P.	Famous Dog Stories	Berk.	.45
————	Big Book of Horse Stories	Berk.	.50
Corbett	Man-Eaters of Kumaon	Ban.	.50
Corbin	High Road Home	Tempo	.50
————	Deadline	Tempo	.50
Cosell	Great Moments in Sports	Macf.	.50
Cousteau	The Silent World	PL	.75
Cousy	Basketball Is My Life	JLP	.50
Crane	The Red Badge of Courage	Dell	.50
Dana	Two Years Before the Mast	Pyr.	.35
Davis	Sex and the Adolescent	Perm.	.50
Defoe	Robinson Crusoe	Dell	.40
Dickens	A Christmas Carol	WSP	.45
————	Great Expectations	WSP	.45
Dikty	5 Tales from Tomorrow	Crest	.50
Dodson	Away All Boats	Ban.	.75
Donovan	PT-109	Crest	.50
Dooley	The Night They Burned the Mountain	Sig.	.60
Dorman	We Shall Overcome	Dell	.75
Douglas	The Robe	PB	.75
Doyle	Study in Scarlet and Sign of the Four	Berk.	.50
————	The Hound of the Baskervilles	Berk.	.50
————	Valley of Fear	Berk.	.50
————	The Lost World	Berk.	.50
Dreiser	An American Tragedy	Sig.	.95

Author	Title	Pub.	Price
Duberman	In White America	Sig.	.60
Dubois	Souls of Black Folk	Crest	.60
Dumas	Count of Monte Cristo	Ban.	.75
Durrell	The Whispering Land	Berk.	.60
————	A Zoo in My Luggage	Berk.	.60
Duvall	Facts of Life and Love for Teenagers	Pop.	.35
————	The Art of Dating	PB	.75
Edmonds	Chad Hanna	Ban.	.75
————	Drums Along the Mohawk	Ban.	.75
Edwards	Strangest of All	Ace	.50
————	Stranger than Science	Ace	.50
————	Strange People	Pop.	.50
Ehrmann	Premarital Dating Behavior	Ban.	.75
Ellis	On Life and Sex	Sig.	.60
Essien-Udom	Black Nationalism	Dell	.75
Falkner	Moon Fleet	Tempo	.50
Felsen	Hot Rod	Ban.	.45
————	Street Rod	Ban.	.45
————	Road Rocket	Ban.	.45
————	Crash Club	Ban.	.45
Fitzgerald	Heroes of Sport	Mac.	.50
Fleming	The Spy Who Loved Me	Sig.	.60
————	Thunderball	Sig.	.60
————	Moonraker	Sig.	.60
————	Casino Royale	Sig.	.60
————	You Only Live Twice	Sig.	.60
————	Goldfinger	Sig.	.60
————	For Your Eyes Only	Sig.	.60
————	Diamonds Are Forever	Sig.	.60
Floren	Deputy's Revenge	pbl	.40
Ford and Berra	The Fighting Southpaw	JLP	.50
Forester	Sink the Bismarck	Ban.	.45
————	The Ship	Ban.	.45
Fort	The Book of the Damned	Ace	.50
Frank	Diary of a Young Girl	PB	.50
Frank	Sea Wolves	Bal.	.75
Friedenberg	The Vanishing Adolescent	Dell	.50
Funk and Lewis	30 Days to a More Powerful Vocabulary	WSP	.60
Furneaux	The World's Strangest Mysteries	Ace	.50
Gaddis	Birdman of Alcatraz	Sig.	.60
Gaer	How the Great Religions Began	Sig.	.60
Gaines	The Mad Sampler	Sig.	.50
Gallico	The Hurricane Story	Berk.	.50
Gann	Fate Is the Hunter	Crest	.75
Garagiola	Baseball Is A Funny Game	Ban.	.40
Gault	Drag Strip	Berk.	.50
————	Speedway Challenge	Berk.	.45
Gibson, A.	I Always Wanted to Be Somebody	Pop.	.60
Gibson, W.	The Miracle Worker	Ban.	.50
Gilbreth	Cheaper by the Dozen	Ban.	.45
Gillette	Inside the Ku Klux Klan	Pyr.	.50
Gipson	Old Yeller	PL	.50
Glazer	New Treasury of Folk Songs	Ban.	.60
Gleeson	Words Most Often Misspelled and Mispronounced	PB	.60
Golden	Mr. Kennedy and the Negroes	Crest	.60
Goodman, I.	Stan Musial	Macf.	.50
Goodman, R. B.	New Ways to Greater Word Power	Dell	.40
Gotlieb	Sunburst	GM	.40
Gottehrer	Basketball Stars of 1965	Pyr.	.50

Author	Title	Pub.	Price
Graham	South Town	Sig.	.50
Graziano	Somebody Up There Likes Me	PB	.35
Gregory	From the Back of the Bus	Avon	.60
Grider	War Fish	Pyr.	.50
Griffin	Black Like Me	Sig.	.60
Grombach	The 1965 Olympic Guide	Avon	.50
Gunther	Death Be Not Proud	PL	.50
Gurney	Five Down and Glory	Bal	.50
Haas	Look Away, Lookaway	PB	.75
Hailey	Runway Zero-Eight	Ban.	.45
Hall	20 Steps to Perfect Spelling	Ban.	.60
Halliday	Shoot to Kill	Dell	.45
————	Call for Mike Shane	Dell	.40
————	Dead Man's Diary	Dell	.40
————	Never Kill a Client	Dell	.40
Hansberry	A Raisin in the Sun	Sig.	.60
Harkins	The Day of the Drag Race	Berk.	.45
	Road Race	SBS	.50
Harmon	Tom Harmon's Book of Sports	JLP	.50
Hawthorne	The Scarlet Letter	Dell	.50
Haycraft	Boys Book of Great Detective Stories	Berk.	.50
	Boys 2nd Book of Great Detective Stories	Berk.	.45
Heinlein	Green Hills of Earth	Sig.	.50
Heise	The Painless Way to Stop Smoking	Crest	.50
Herndon	Humor of J.F.K.	GM	.50
Hersey	Hiroshima	Ban.	.50
	The Wall	PB	.75
Heyerdahl	Kon-Tiki	PB	.75
	Aku-Aku	PB	.75
Hilton	Lost Horizon	PB	.50
Himes	The Primitive	Sig.	.60
	The Third Generation	Sig.	.75
Hirsch	Great Untold Stories of WW II	Pyr.	.50
	Killer Subs	Pyr.	.50
Hitchcock	Stories My Mother Never Told Me	Dell	.50
	Fourteen Suspense Stories to Play Russian Roulette	Dell	.50
Horsley	The Hot Rod Handbook	JLP	.75
Howarth	We Die Alone	Ace	.40
	D Day	Pyr.	.50
Hugo	Hunchback of Notre Dame	Ban.	.60
Hunter	Blackboard Jungle	PB	.50
Huxley	Brave New World	Ban.	.60
Hyman	No Time for Sergeants	Sig.	.60
Icenhower	The Scarlet Raider	Nova	.40
Irving	Legend of Sleepy Hollow	WSP	.60
Jacobs	Korea's Heroes	Berk.	.35
James	Ghosts and Things	Berk.	.50
Jones	High Gear	Ban.	.50
Kantor	If the South Had Won the Civil War	Ban.	.45
	Andersonville	Sig.	.95
Kaplan	More Posers	Macf.	.50
Karloff	Favorite Horror Stories	Avon	.50
Kennedy	Profiles in Courage	PL	.65
Ketchum	Dennis the Menace—Make Believe Angel	Crest	.35
————	Dennis the Menace, Household Hurricane	Crest	.35
————	In This Corner . . . Dennis the		

Author	Title	Pub.	Price
	Menace	Crest	.35
———	Dennis the Menace Rides Again	Crest	.35
———	Dennis the Menace vs. Everybody	Crest	.35
———	Wanted, Dennis the Menace	Crest	.35
King	Strength to Love	PB	.50
———	Stride Toward Freedom	PL	.65
———	Why We Can't Wait	Sig.	.60
Kipling	The Jungle Books	Sig.	.50
———	Captains Courageous	Dell	.35
———	Kim	Dell	.40
Knebel	No High Ground	Ban.	.50
Knight	Tomorrow X4	GM	.50
Koh	Divided Family	Berk.	.35
Krich	Facts of Love and Marriage for Young People	Dell	.50
Kytle	Willie Mae	Sig.	.50
Lafarge	Laughing Boy	PB	.35
Lamb	Genghis Khan	Ban.	.60
Landers	Ann Landers Talks to Teenagers About Sex	Crest	.40
Laumer	A Trace of Memory	Berk.	.50
Lederer and Burdick	Ugly American	Crest	.50
Lee	To Kill a Mockingbird	Pop.	.60
Leiber	The Wanderer	Bal.	.75
Leinster	The Other Side of Nowhere	Berk.	.50
———	Invaders of Space	Berk.	.50
———	Four From Planet 5	GM	.40
Lewis, C.	Adam Clayton Powell	GM	.40
Lewis, N.	Rapid Vocabulary Builder	Macf.	.75
Ley	Satellites, Rockets and Outer Space	NAL	.60
Liebers	Wit's End	Tempo	.50
Lomax	The Negro Revolt	Sig.	.75
———	When the Word Is Given	Sig.	.60
London	Call of the Wild; White Fang	Ban.	.45
———	The Sea Wolf	Ban.	.50
Lord	Day of Infamy	Ban.	.50
———	A Night to Remember	Ban.	.45
Maddox	How to Study	Crest	.60
Mantle	Quality of Courage	Ban.	.50
Margulies	Get Out of My Sky	Crest	.45
———	The Ghoul Keepers	Pyr.	.50
Marquand	Think Fast, Mr. Moto	Berk.	.50
Martin	W.W. II in Pictures	GM	.60
Masin	Great Sports Stories	Berk.	.40
Maury	The Good War	Macf.	.75
Maxwell	Ring of Bright Water	Crest	.60
May	The Wasted Americans	Sig.	.60
McCormick	The Five Man Break	Nova	.40
McCutchan	Bluebolt One	Berk.	.50
McKay	Home to Harlem	PB	.50
McWhirter	Guinness Book of World Records	Ban.	.95
Melville	Billy Budd	Ban.	.50
———	Moby Dick	Sig.	.75
Merriam	Battle of the Bulge	Bal.	.60
Michener	Bridges at Toko-Ri	Ban.	.40
———	Bridge at Andau	Ban.	.45
———	Hawaii	Ban.	.95
Miller, A. G.	Fury	Tempo	.50
Miller, R. D.	Stranger Than Life	Ace	.50
———	Impossible, Yet It Happened	Ace	.40
Miller, W.	The Siege of Harlem	Crest	.60

Author	Title	Pub.	Price
————	The Cool World	Crest	.40
Mitchell	The Amazing Mets	Tempo	.50
Monsarrat	The Cruel Sea	PB	.75
Montagu	The Man Who Never Was	Ban.	.45
Morehead	Official Rules of Card Games	Crest	.60
Morrow	Black Man in the White House	Macf.	.60
Neider	Man Against Nature	Ban.	.50
Newcombe	Floyd Patterson	Macf.	.50
Nordhoff and Hall	Men Against the Sea	PB	.35
————	Pitcairn's Island	PB	.35
Nordholt	The People That Walk in Darkness	Bal.	.75
Norton	Time Traders	Ace	.40
————	Defiant Agents	Ace	.40
————	Witch World	Ace	.40
————	Sea Siege and Eye of the Monster	Ace	.40
O'Connor, P.	The Black Tiger	Berk.	.45
————	Treasure at Twenty Fathoms	Berk.	.50
Orwell	Animal Farm	Sig.	.75
Owen, D.	The Latchy Gun	Avon	.40
Owen, F.	Baseball Stories	PB	.50
Pangborn	Davy	Bal.	.75
Papashvily	Anything Can Happen	PL	.50
Paradis	From High School to a Job	Avon	.50
Parks	The Learning Tree	Crest	.60
Pinto	Spy Catcher	Berk.	.60
Poe	Fall of the House of Usher	NAL	.50
Porter	Winning Pitcher	Tempo	.50
————	"Keeper" Play	Tempo	.50
Pratt	Pro, Pro, Pro	JLP	.50
Purdy	The Kings of the Road	Ban.	.75
Quarles	The Negro in the Making of America	Collr.	.95
Queen	To Be Read Before Midnight	Pop.	.50
Raab	American Race Relations Today	Anch.	.95
Rascovich	The Bedford Incident	PB	.75
Rawicz	The Long Walk	PL	.60
Reading Lab.	Double Your Reading Speed	Crest	.60
Redding	On Being Negro in America	Ban.	.60
Reeder	West Point Plebe	Berk.	.45
————	West Point Yearling	Berk.	.50
Reid	Escape from Colditz	Berk.	.50
Remarque	All Quiet on the Western Front	Crest	.50
Reynolds	Officially Dead	Pyr.	.40
————	70,000 to One	Pyr.	.50
————	They Fought for the Sky	Ban.	.50
Richter	Light in the Forest	Ban.	.45
Robinson	Baseball Stars of 1965	Crest	.75
Roberts	Captain Caution	Pyr.	.50
Rohmer	Island of Fu Manchu	Pyr.	.40
————	The Day the World Ended	Ace	.40
————	Inside Dr. Fu Manchu	Pyr.	.40
————	Mask of Fu Manchu	Pyr.	.50
Rosen	But Not Next Door	Avon	.50
Rosten	Captain Newman, M.D.	Crest	.60
Rostand	Cyrano de Bergerac	Ban.	.50
Ruppelt	Report on U.F.O.	Ace	.50
Russell, E. F.	Men, Martians and Machines	Berk.	.50
Ryan	The Longest Day	Crest	.50
Salisbury	The Shook-Up Generation	Crest	.50
Schaefer	Shane	Ban.	.45
Schultz	My Life as an Indian	Prem.	.60

Author	Title	Pub.	Price
Schulz	For the Love of Peanuts	Crest	.40
————	Fun With Peanuts	Crest	.40
————	Good Grief, Charlie Brown	Crest	.40
————	Here Comes Charlie Brown	Crest	.35
Scoggin	Chucklebait	Dell	.50
Scott	Ivanhoe	PB	.75
Serling	Stories from the Twilight Zone	Ban.	.45
————	More Stories from the Twilight Zone	Ban.	.45
————	New Stories from the Twilight Zone	Ban.	.45
————	Rod Serling's Triple W	Ban.	.50
————	Requiem for a Heavyweight	Ban.	.40
Sewell	Black Beauty	Airmt.	.50
Scheckley	Citizen in Space	Bal.	.50
Shelley	Frankenstein	Dell	.45
Short	King Colt	Ban.	.40
Shotwell	Roosevelt Grady	Tempo	.50
Shulman, I.	West Side Story	PB	.50
Shulman, M.	I Was A Teen-Age Dwarf	Ban.	.50
————	The Many Loves of Dobie Gillis	Ban.	.50
————	Rally Round the Flag, Boys	Ban.	.75
Silverberg	Sunken History	Macf.	.60
Silverman	Best from Sport	Ban.	.50
Simak	Way Station	Macf.	.50
	Time Is the Simplest Thing	Crest	.50
Simmons	So You Think You Know Baseball	Crest	.40
Sloane	How You Can Forecast the Weather	Prem.	.60
Smith	The Quarterbacks	JLP	.50
Smythe	Meet Andy Capp	GM	.40
Snelling	007 James Bond: A Report	Sig.	.50
Stanford	The Red Car	Tempo	.50
Stainback	Football Stars of 1965	Pyr.	.50
Steinbeck	The Red Pony	Ban.	.45
	The Pearl	Ban.	.45
————	East of Eden	Ban.	.95
————	The Grapes of Wrath	Ban.	.95
————	Sweet Thursday	Ban.	.75
————	The Moon Is Down	Ban.	.50
————	Of Mice and Men	Ban.	.50
————	Cannery Row	Ban.	.50
Stern	Great Ghost Stories	WSP	.60
Stevenson	Kidnapped	Dell	.40
Stuart	Satan Bug	Pop.	.50
Summers	Trouble on the Run	Tempo	.50
Tregaskis	Guadalcanal Diary	Pop.	.40
	Vietnam Diary	Pop.	.60
Trevor-Roper	The Last Days of Hitler	Collr.	.95
Trimble	Yogi Berra	Tempo	.50
Trumbell	The Raft	Pyr.	.45
Tunis	Schoolboy Johnson	Berk.	.45
————	Young Razzle	Berk.	.45
————	World Series	Berk.	.50
————	Silence Over Dunkerque	Berk.	.50
Twain	Life on the Mississippi	Ban.	.50
————	Adventures of Tom Sawyer	Dell	.40
————	Mysterious Stranger and Other Stories	Sig.	.50
————	A Connecticut Yankee	WSP	.45
————	The Prince and the Pauper	PL	.50
————	Roughing It	NAL	.75
————	Adventures of Huckleberry Finn	WSP	.45
Uris	Exodus	Ban.	.95
————	Battle Cry	Ban.	.95

Author	Title	Pub.	Price
Van Every	A Company of Heroes	Mentor	.75
Van Vogt	Mission to the Stars	Berk.	.50
———	Destination: Universe!	Berk.	.50
———	Away and Beyond	Berk.	.50
Verne	20,000 Leagues Under the Sea	Ban.	.60
———	Journey to the Center of the Earth	Perm.	.35
———	Master of the World	Ace	.35
———	The Mysterious Island	Perm.	.60
Verrill	The Strange Story of our Earth	Prem.	.50
Villiers	Great Sea Stories	Dell	.45
Wadsworth	Puzzle of the Talking Monkey	Tempo	.50
Waldman	Challenger	Tempo	.50
Waldron and Gleeson	The Frogmen	Berk.	.50
Walters	First on the Moon	Tempo	.50
Washington	Up from Slavery	Ban.	.60
Waters	His Eye Is on the Sparrow	Ban.	.75
Wells, H. G.	Island of Dr. Moreau	Berk.	.45
———	War of the Worlds	Sig.	.75
———	Invisible Man	Berk.	.50
———	The Time Machine	Berk.	.50
———	The Inexperienced Ghost	Berk.	.45
Wells, L. E.	Brand of Evil	Ban.	.50
Westheimer	Von Ryan's Express	Berk.	.40
White	Teen-Age Dance Book	Perm.	.50
Whitehead	F.B.I. Story	PB	.75
Whitman	Captain Apache	Berk.	.45
Williams, E.	The Tunnel Escape	Berk.	.50
Williams, O.	New Pocket Anthology of Am. Verse	WSP	.75
———	Major American Poets	Mentor	.95
———	Immortal Poems of the English Language	WSP	.75
Wouk	City Boy	Dell	.60
Wright	Black Boy	Sig.	.75
———	Native Son	Sig.	.75
———	The Outsider	PL	.95
———	Uncle Tom's Children	PL	.60
———	White Man Listen	Anch.	.95
Wyss	Swiss Family Robinson	Dell	.40
Young	Rommel, The Desert Fox	PL	.60
Zanger	Pro Football—1965	PB	.95
Zinkoff	Go Man Go	Pyr.	.35

PUBLISHERS AND SYMBOLS

Ace   Ace Books and Ace Star Books, 1120 Avenue of the Americas, New York, N.Y. 10036

Airmt.   Airmont Publishing Co., Inc., 22 E. 60th Street, New York, N.Y. 10022

Anch.   Anchor Books, Doubleday & Co., Inc., 277 Park Avenue, New York, N.Y. 10017

Avon   Avon Book Div., The Hearst Corp., 959 Eighth Avenue, New York, N.Y. 10019

Bal.   Ballantine Books, Inc., 101 Fifth Avenue, New York, N.Y. 10003

Ban.   Bantam Books, Inc., 271 Madison Avenue, New York, N.Y. 10016

Berk.   Berkley Publishing Corp., 15 E. 26th Street, New York, N.Y. 10010

Cllr.   Collier Books, 60 Fifth Avenue, New York, N.Y. 10003

Crest   Crest Books, Fawcett Publications, Inc., Greenwich, Conn. 06830

Dell Dell Publishing Co., Inc., 750 Third Avenue, New York, N.Y. 10017

GM Gold Medal Books, Fawcett Publications, Inc. Greenwich, Conn. 06830

JLP J. Lowell Pratt & Co., 15 E. 48th Street, New York, N.Y. 10017

Macf. Macfadden Books, Macfadden-Bartell Corp., 205 E. 42nd Street, New York, N.Y. 10017

Ment. Mentor Books *see* NAL

NAL New American Library of World Literature, Inc., 1301 Avenue of the Americas, New York, N.Y. 10019

Nova Nova Books, Universal Publishing & Distributing Corp., 800 Second Avenue, New York, N.Y. 10017

PB Pocket Books, Inc., 630 Fifth Avenue, New York, N.Y. 10020

pbl Paperback Library, Inc., 260 Park Avenue South, New York, N.Y. 10010

Perm. Permabooks *see* PB

PL Perennial Library, Harper & Row, Publishers, 49 E. 33rd Street, New York, N.Y. 10016

Pop. Popular Library, Inc., 355 Lexington Avenue, New York, N.Y. 10017

Prem. Premier Books, Fawcett Publications, Inc., Greenwich, Conn. 06830

Pyr. Pyramid Books, Pyramid Publications, Inc., 444 Madison Avenue, New York, N.Y. 10022

SBS Scholastic Book Services, 900 Sylvan Avenue, Englewood Cliffs, N.J.

Sig. Signet Books *see* NAL

Tempo Tempo Books, Grosset & Dunlap, Inc., 51 Madison Avenue, New York, N.Y. 10010

WSP Washington Square Press, Inc., 630 Fifth Avenue, New York, N.Y. 10020